RELAXING
Coloring Book 1

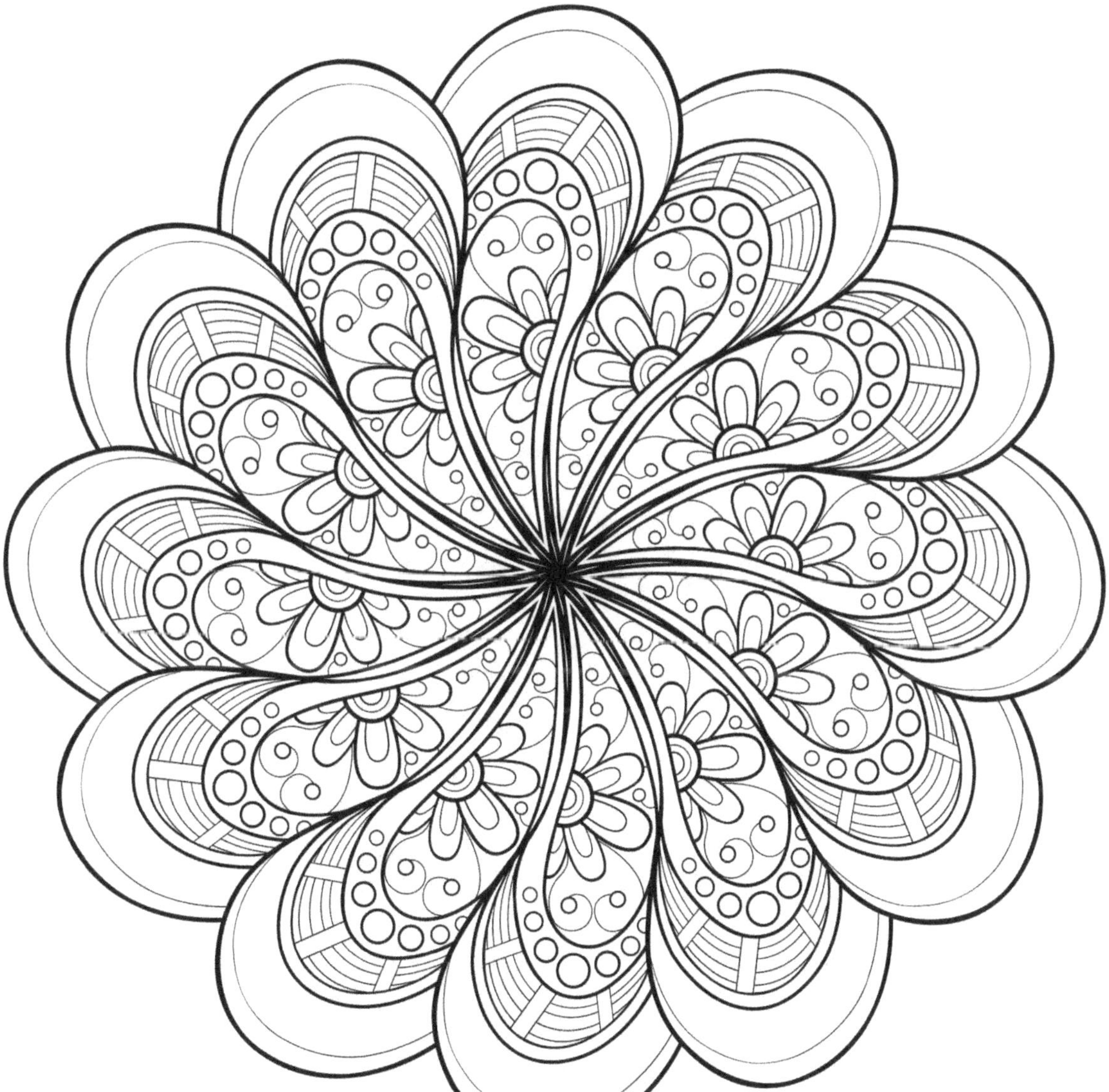

V ART

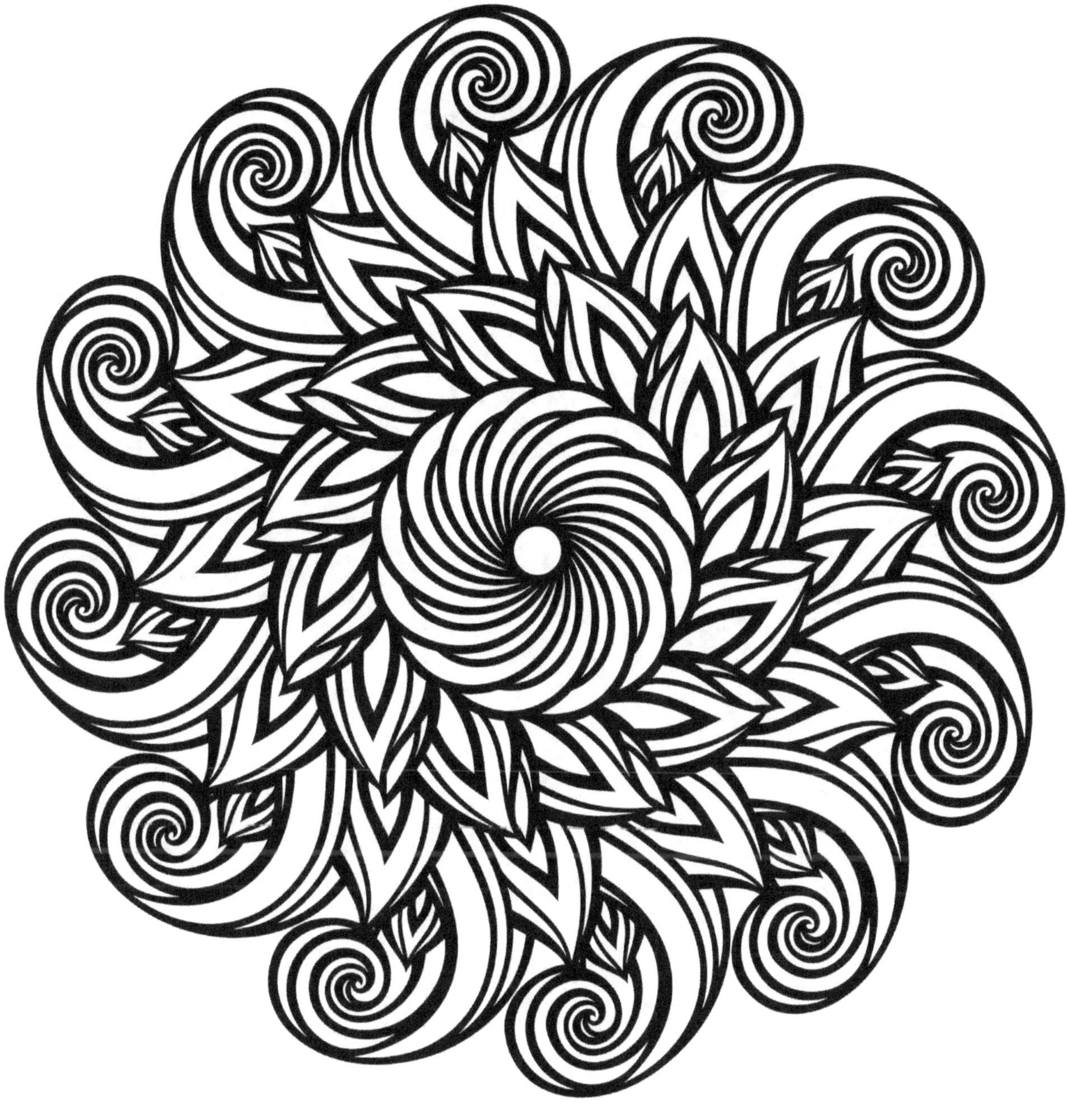

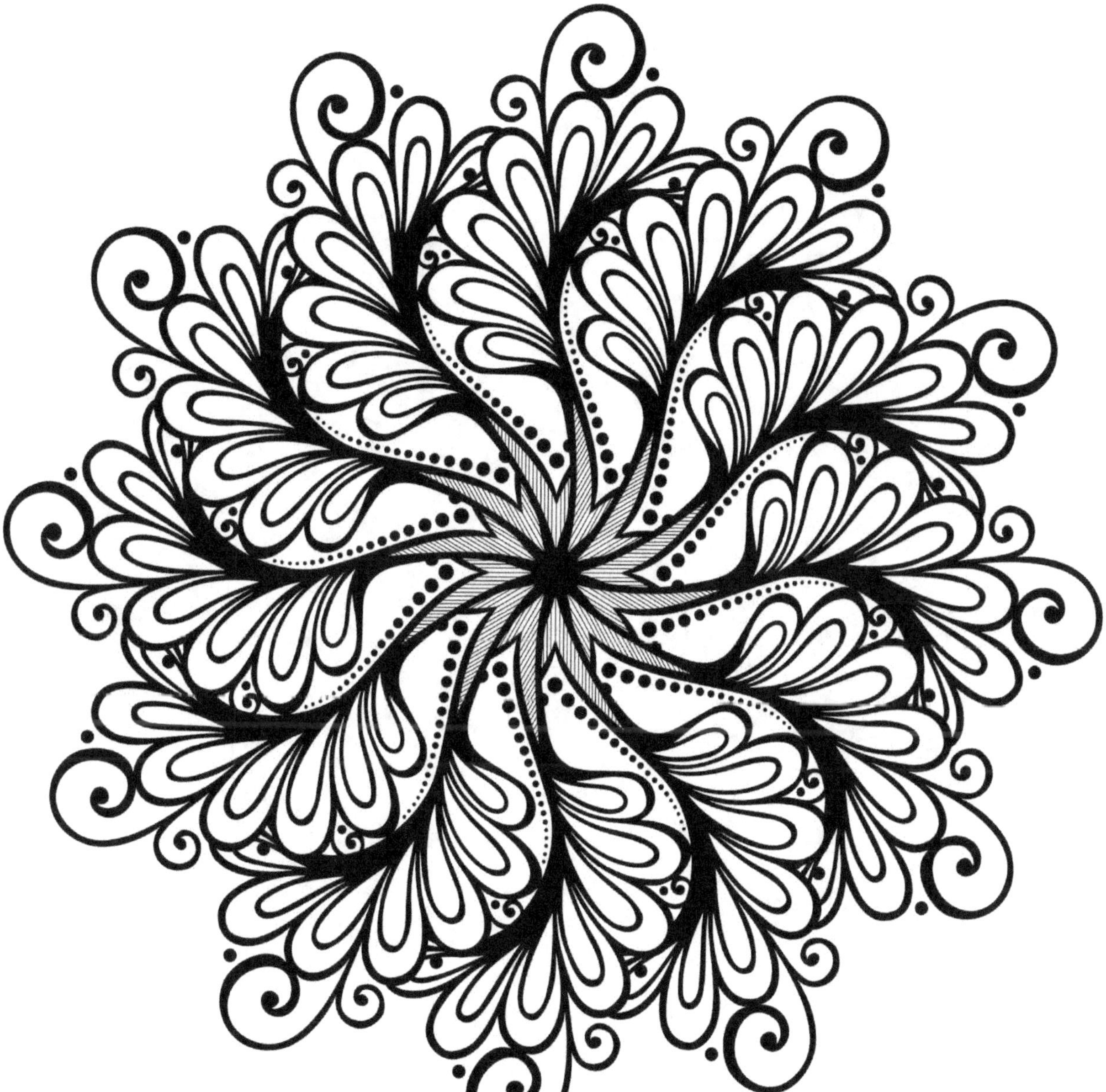

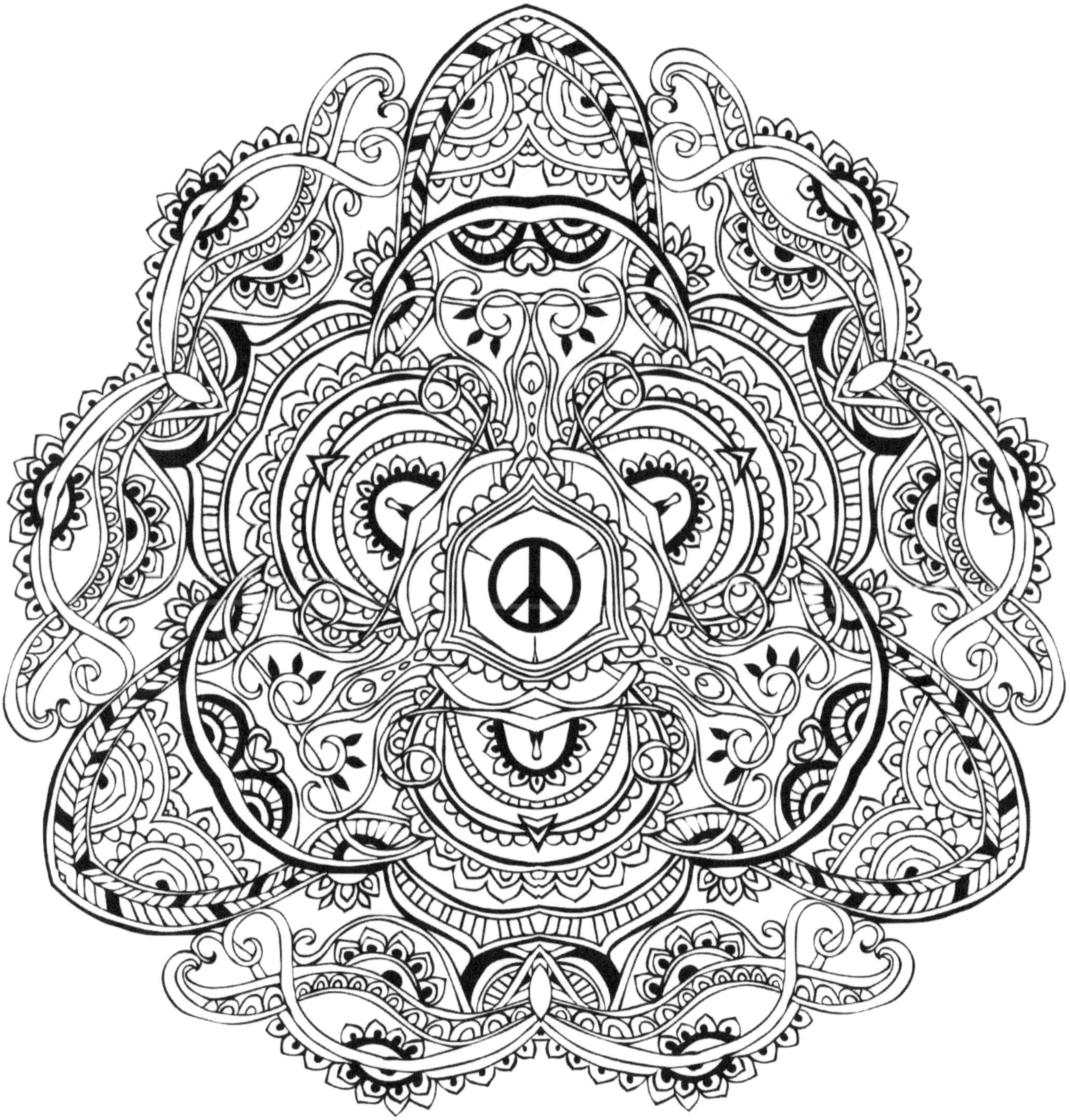

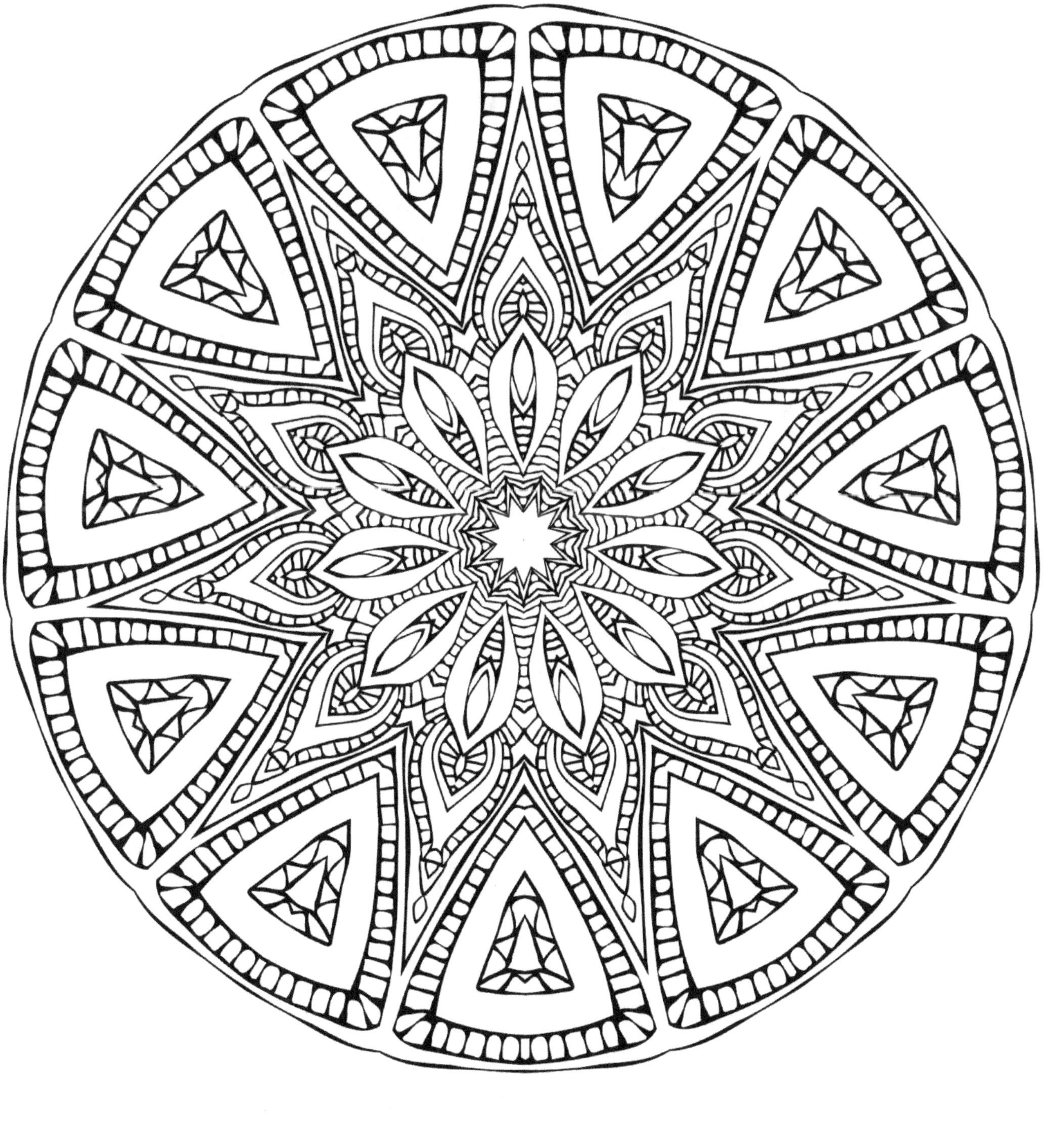

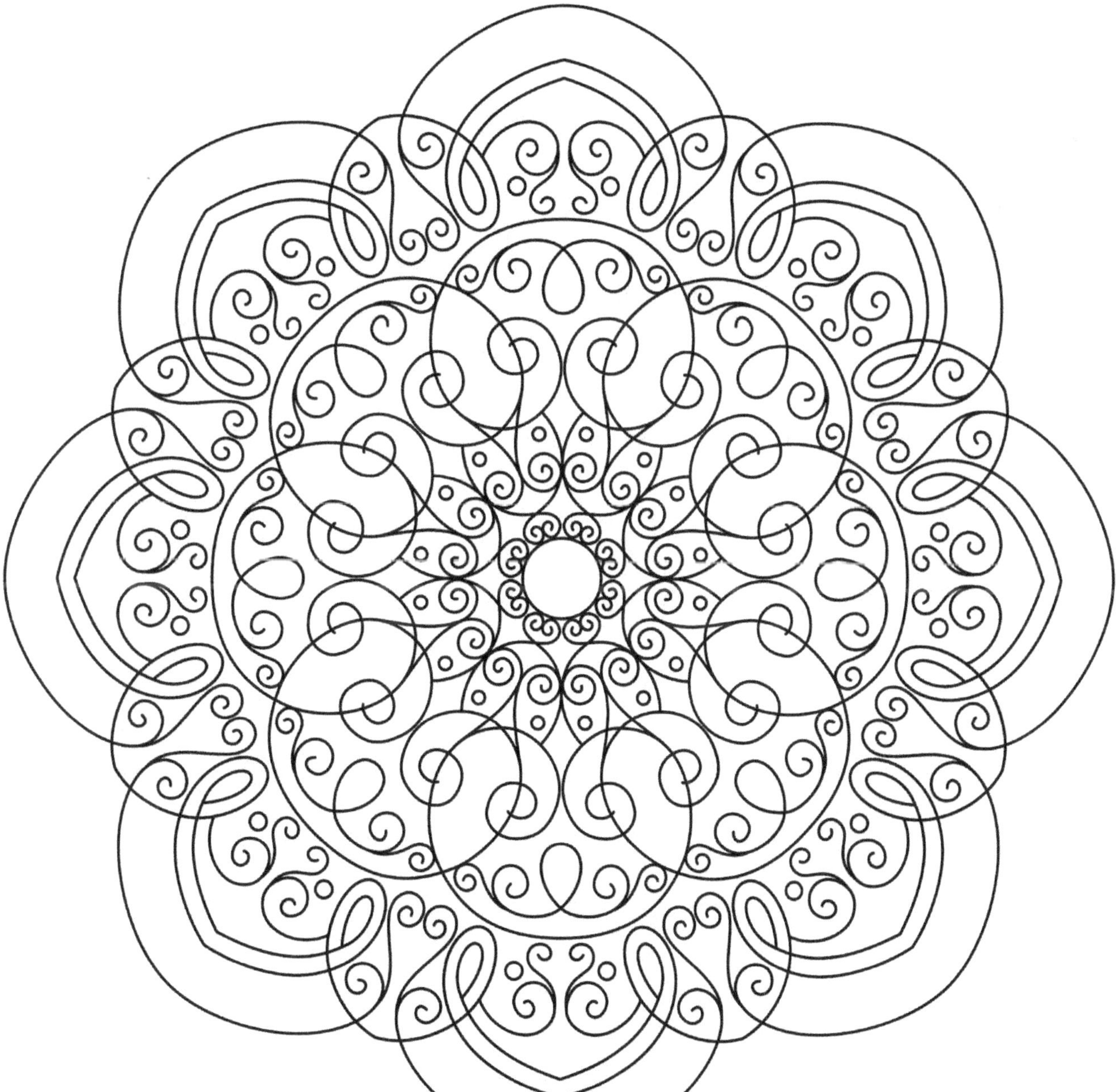

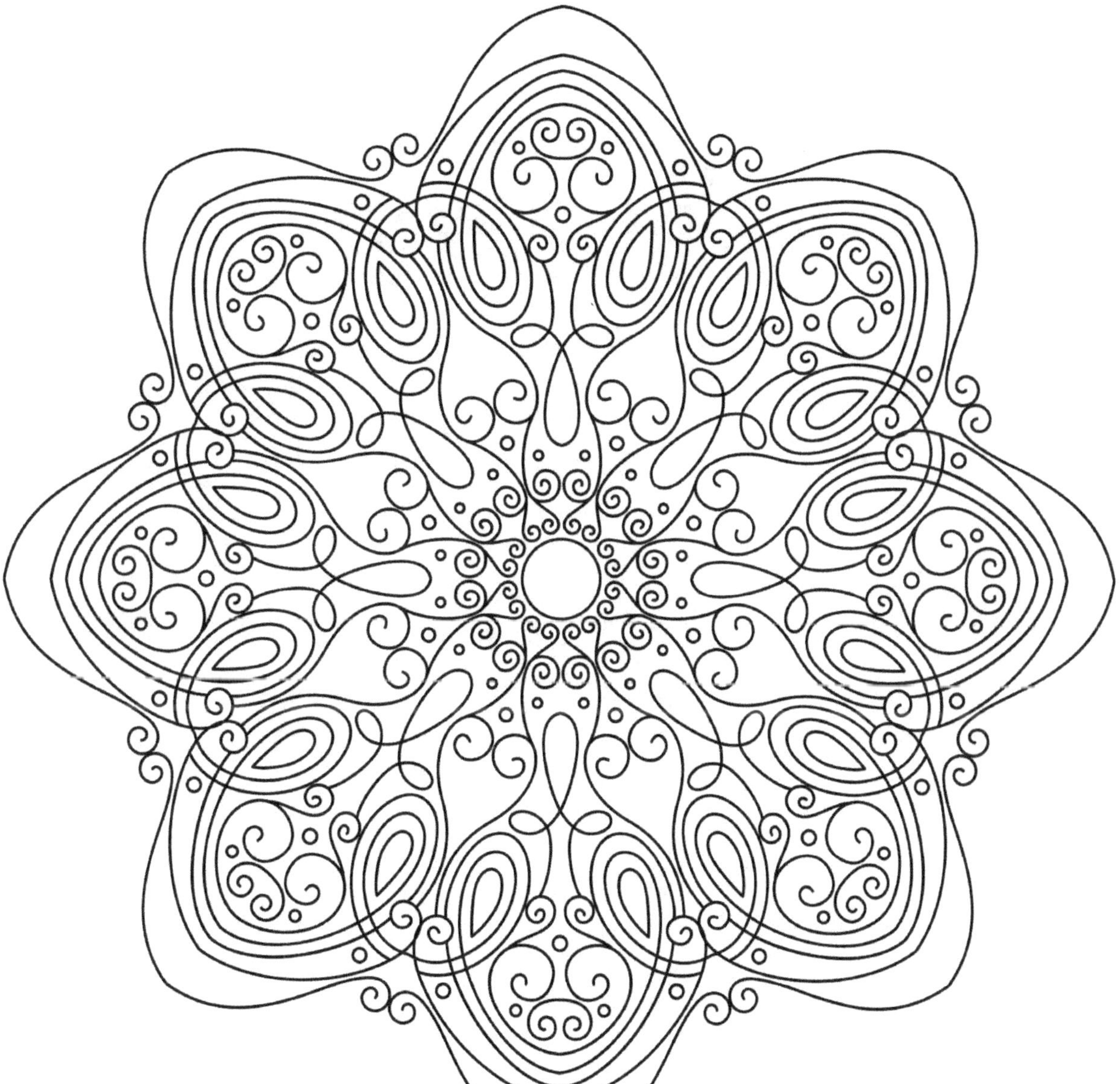

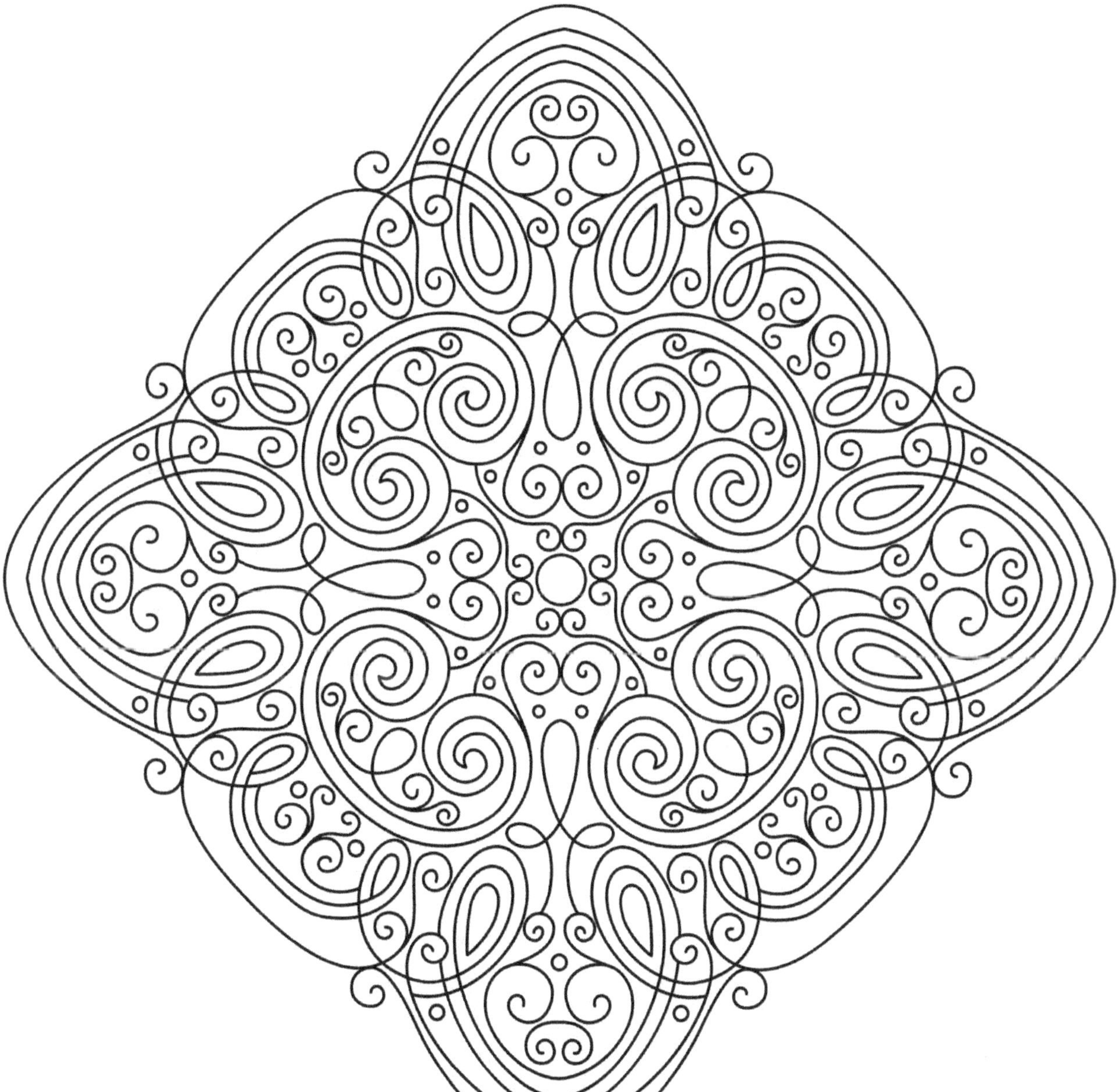

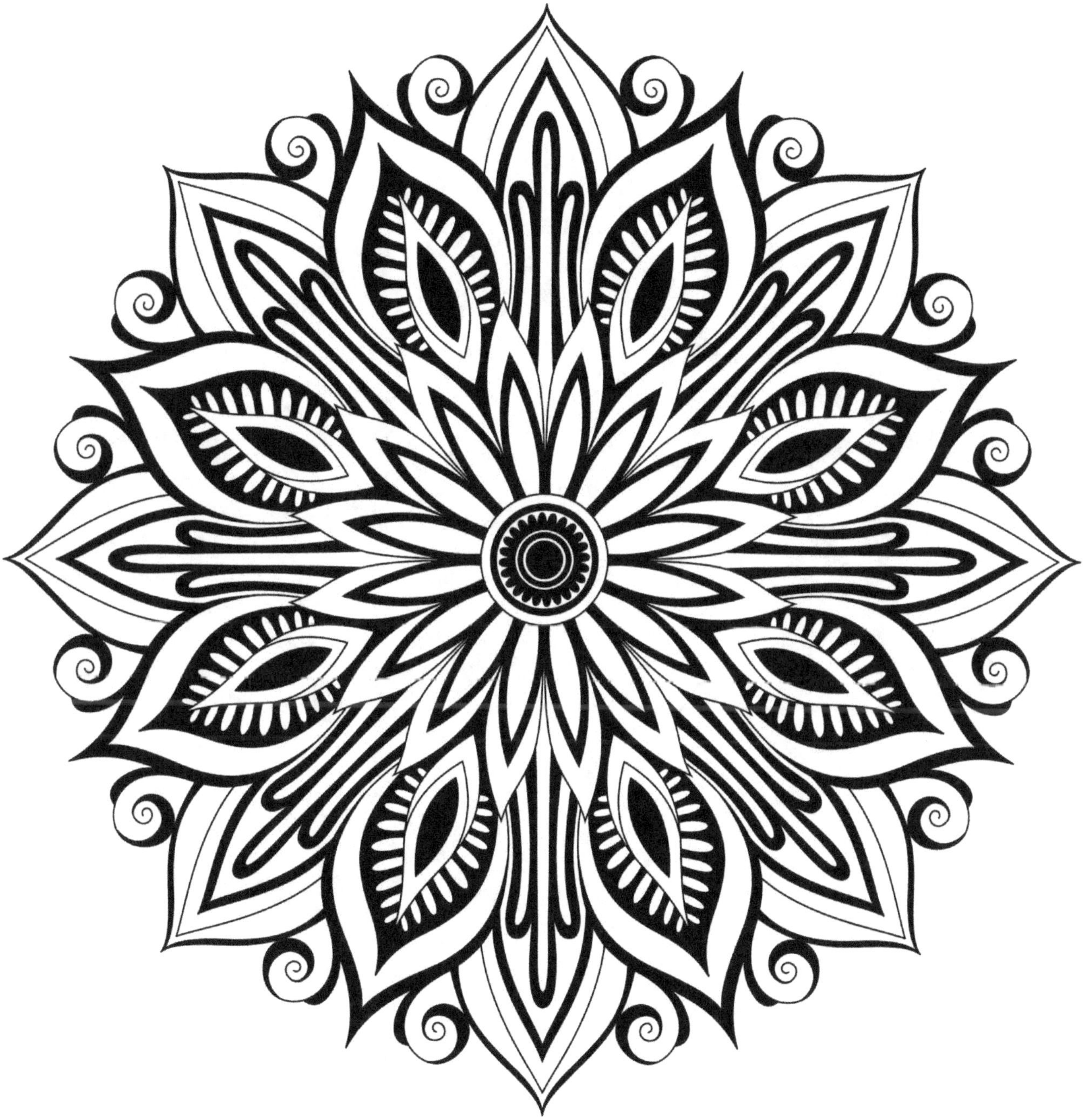

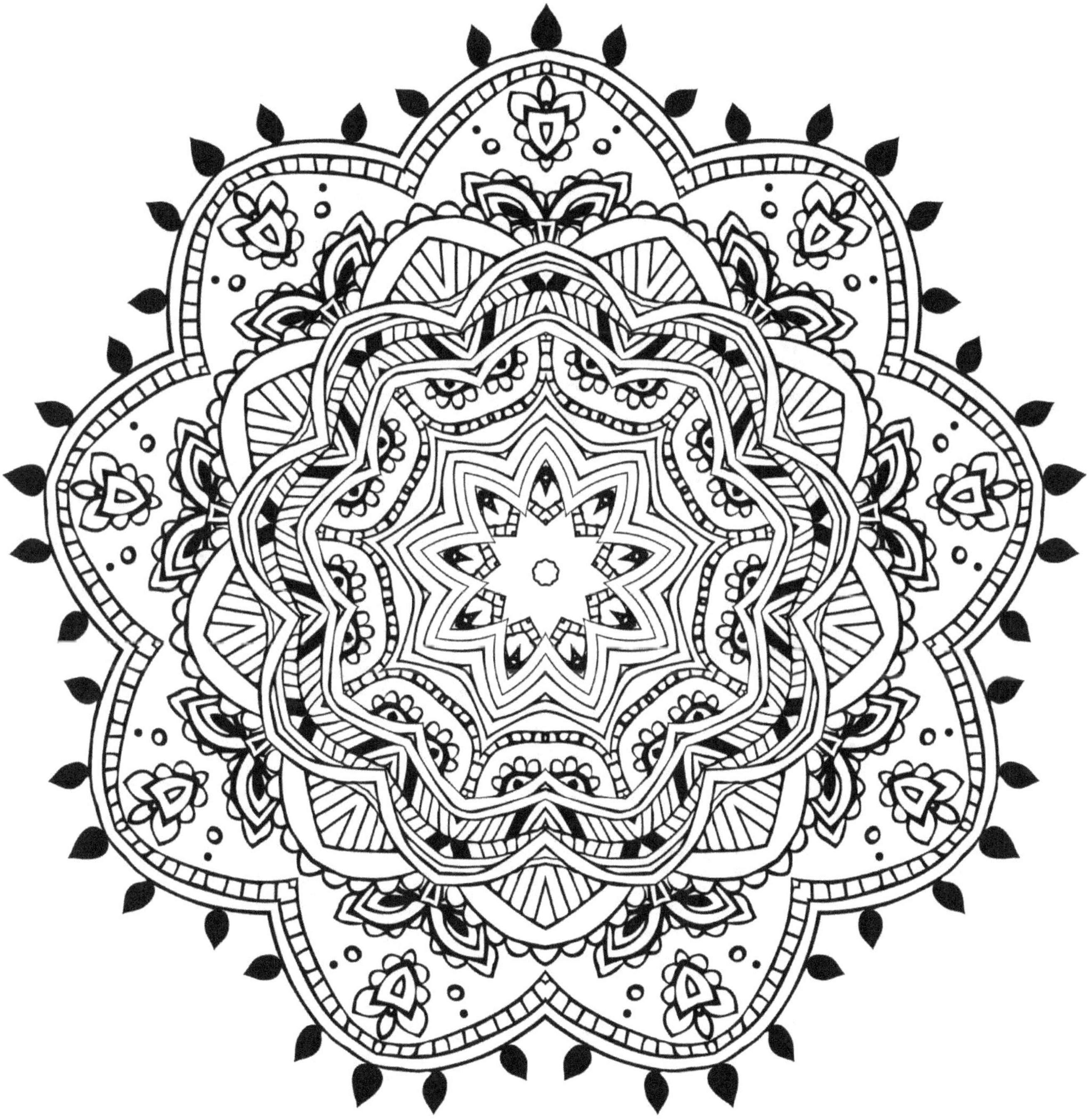

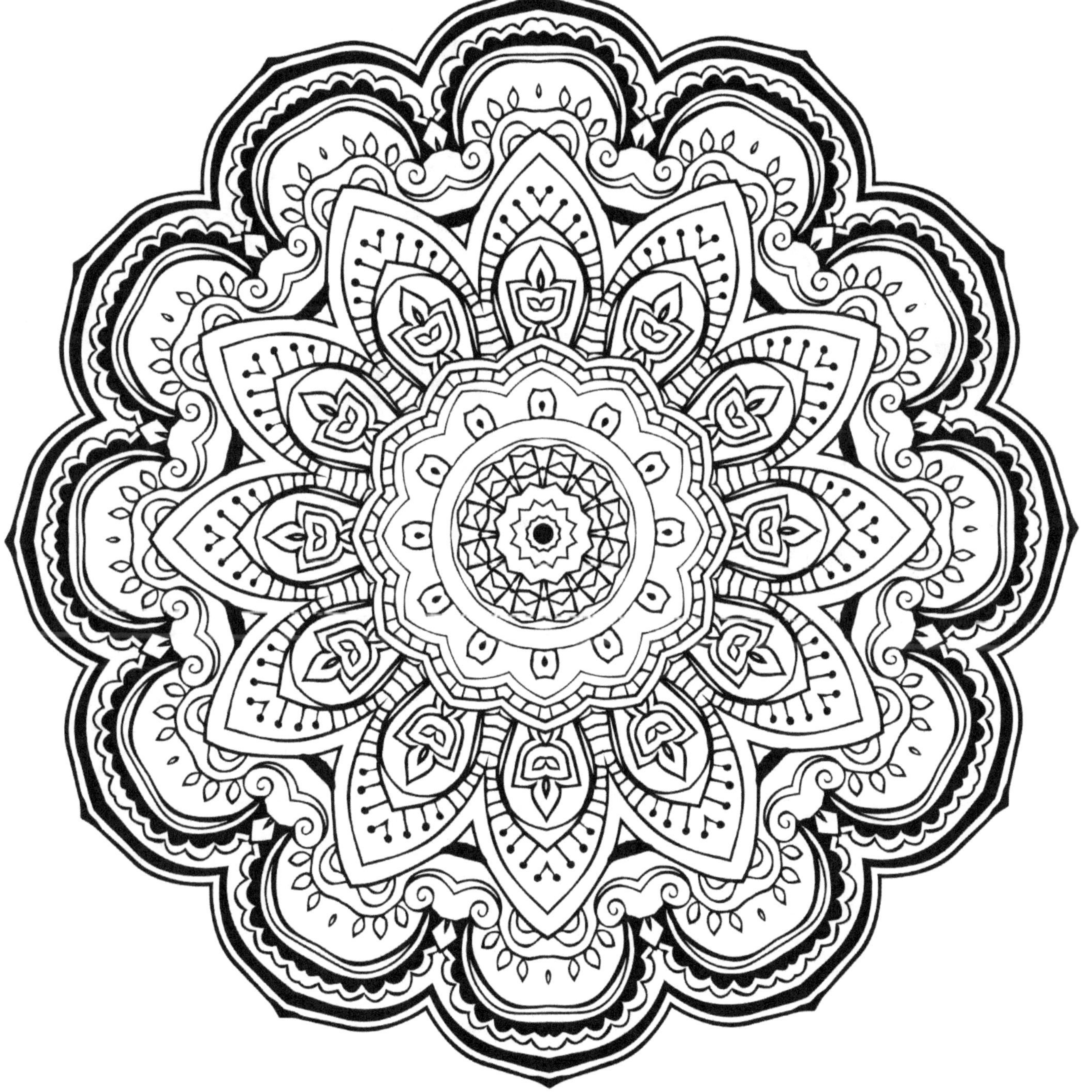

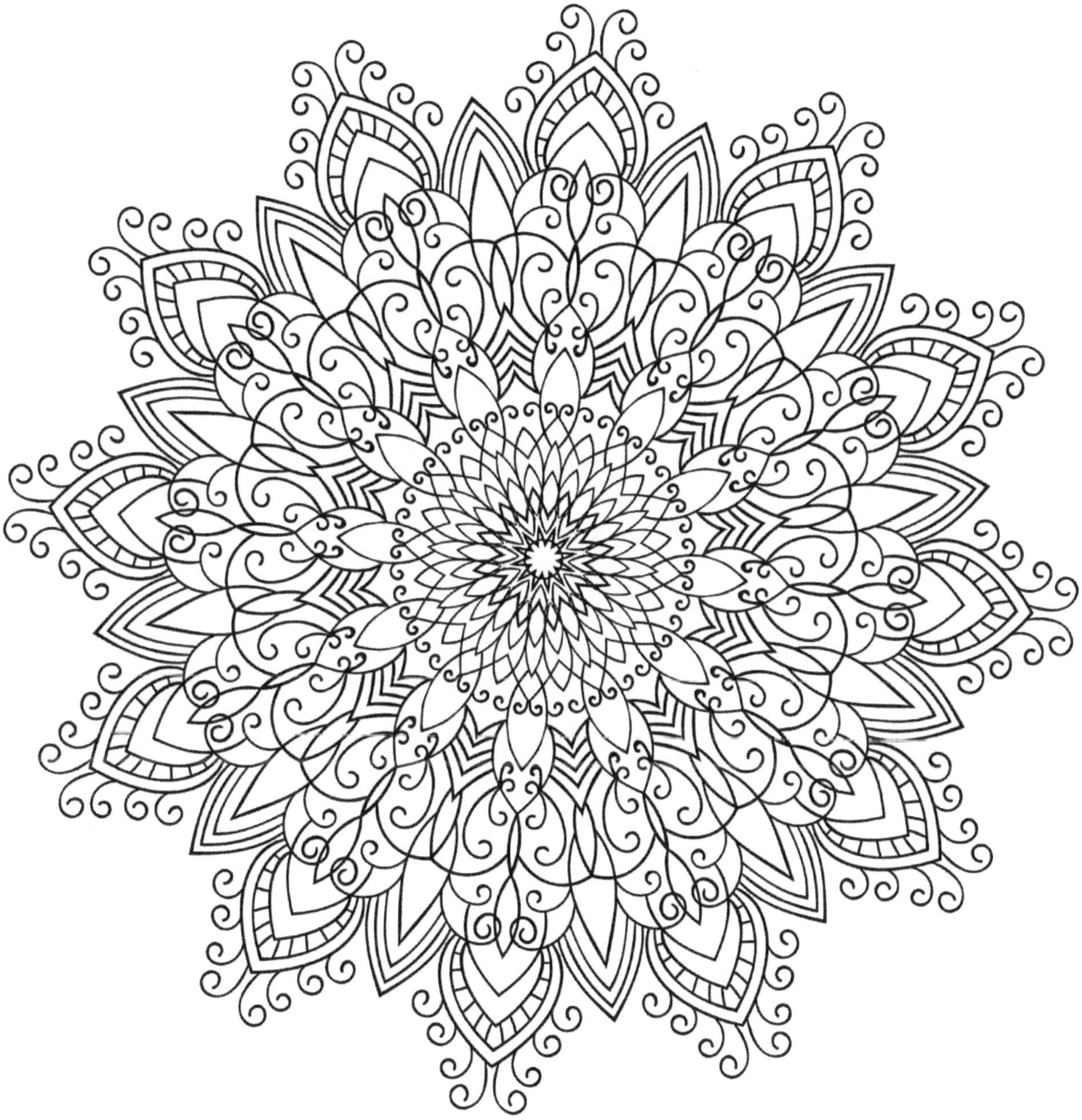

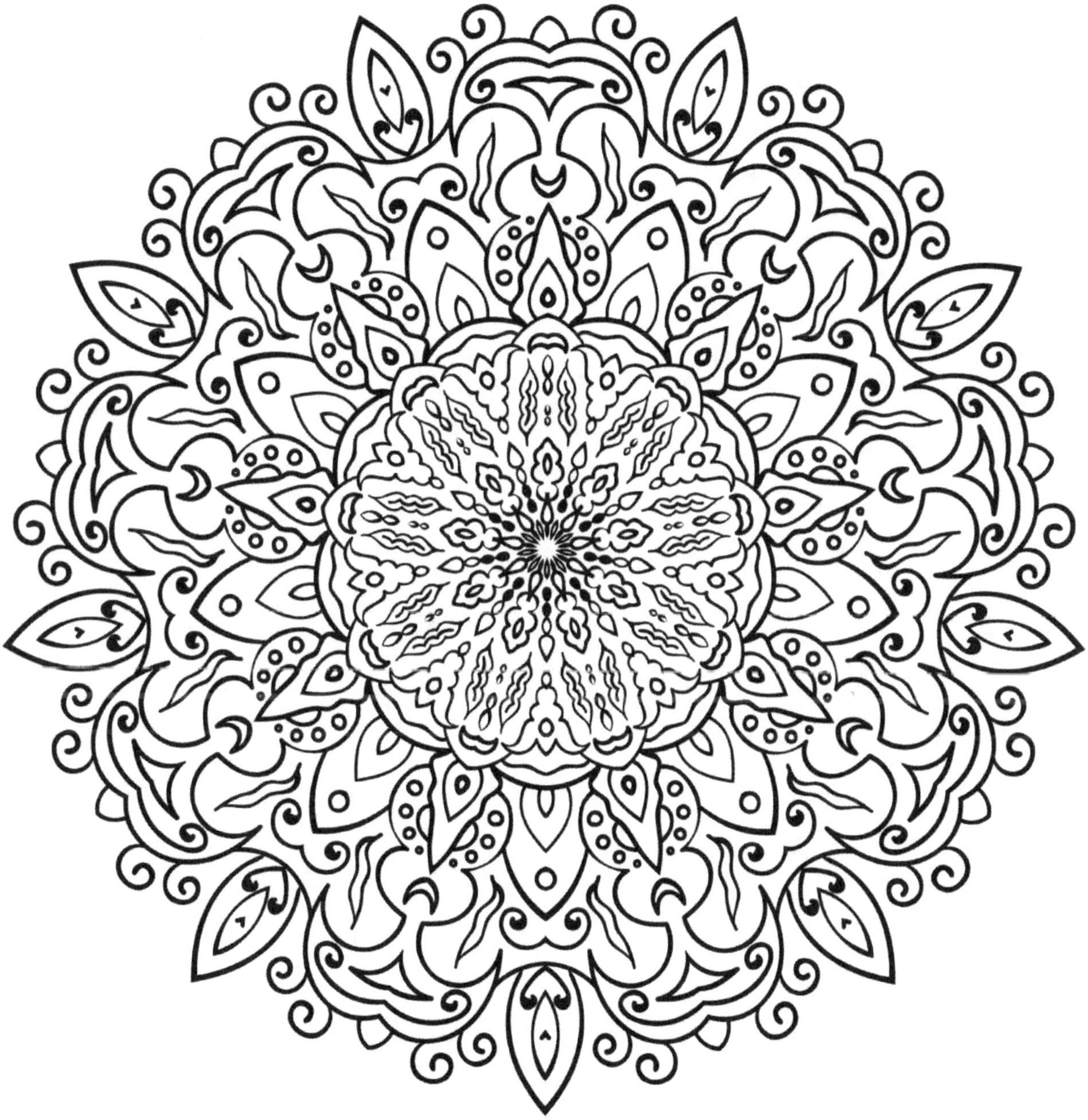

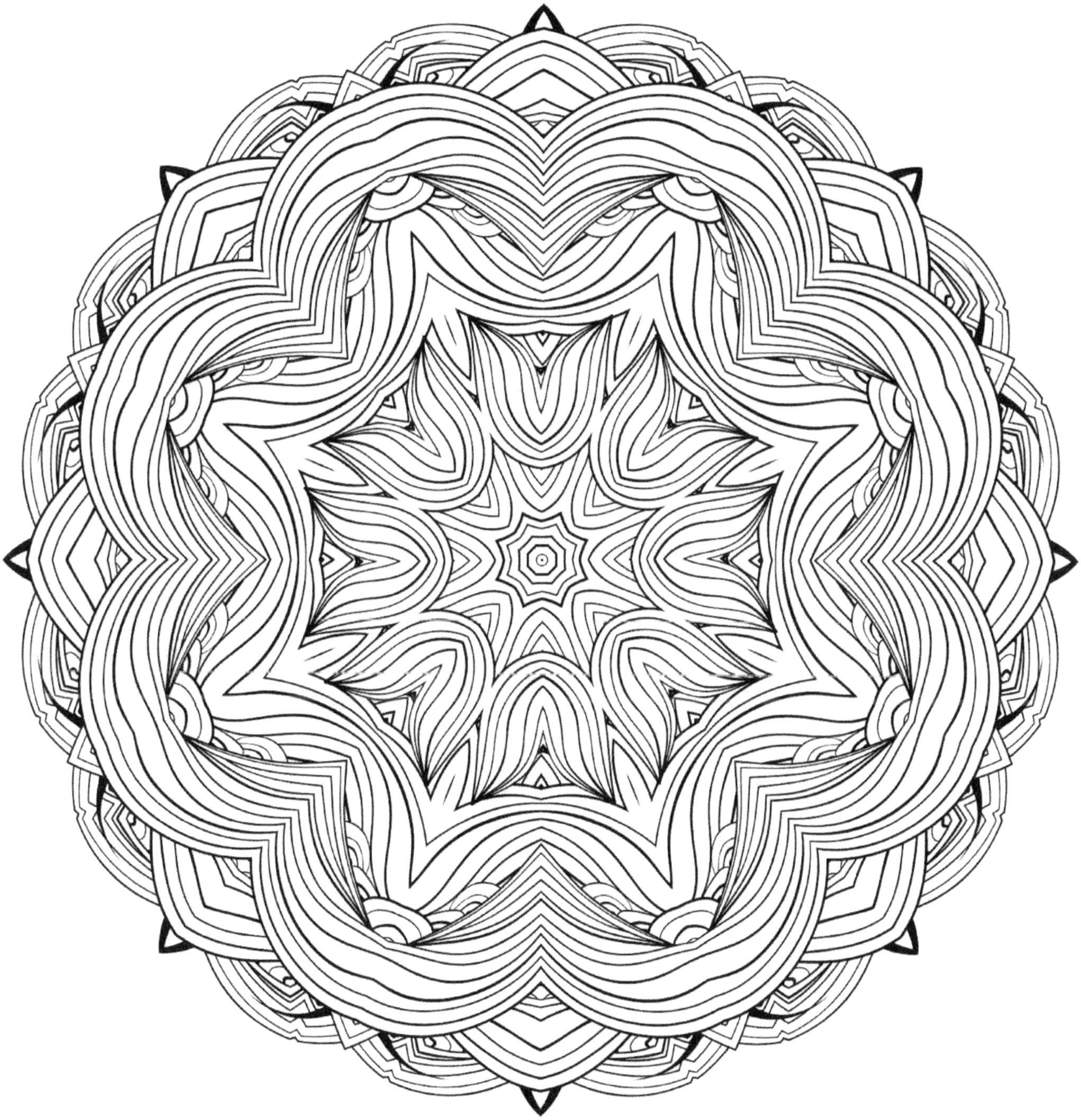

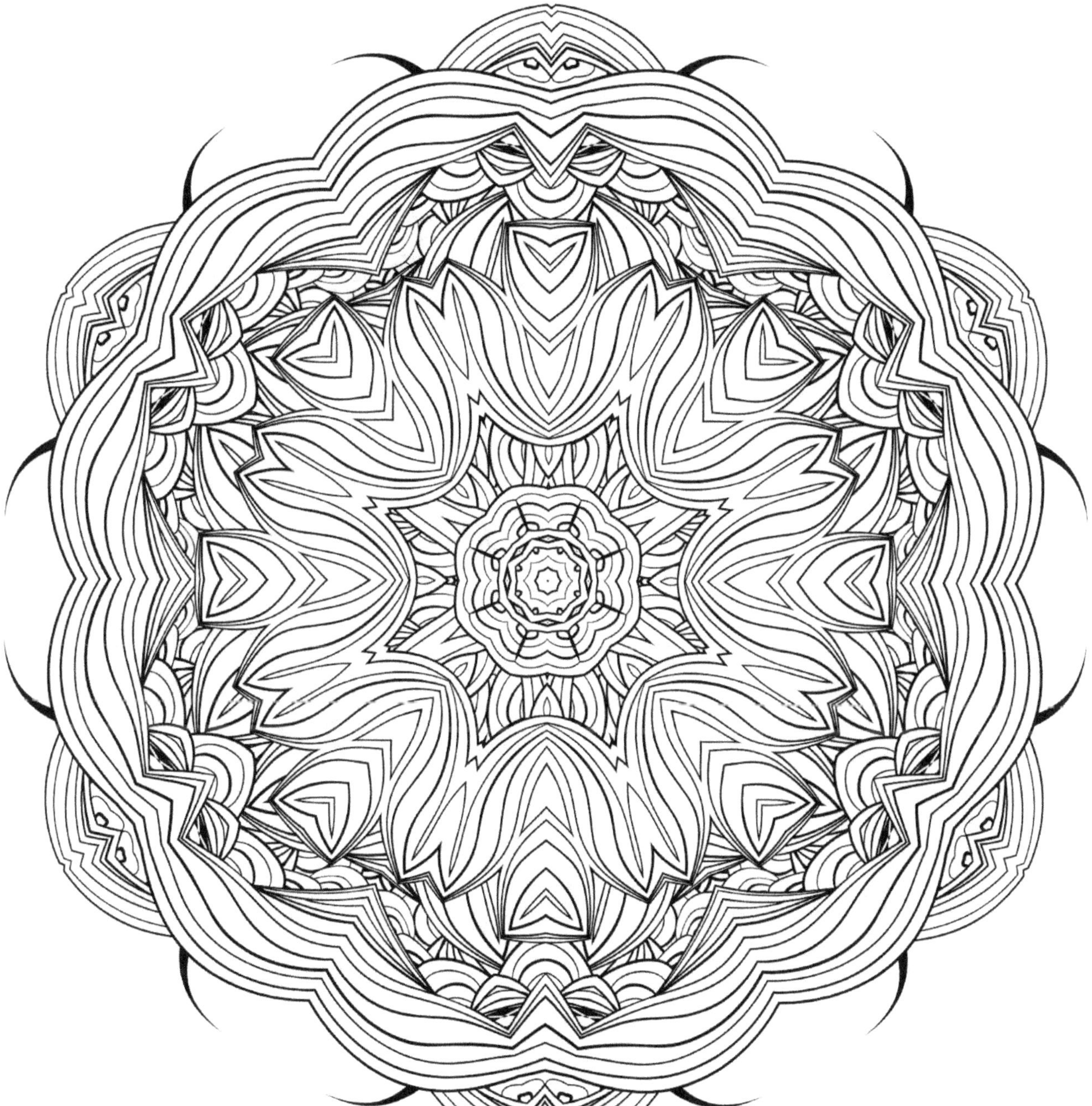

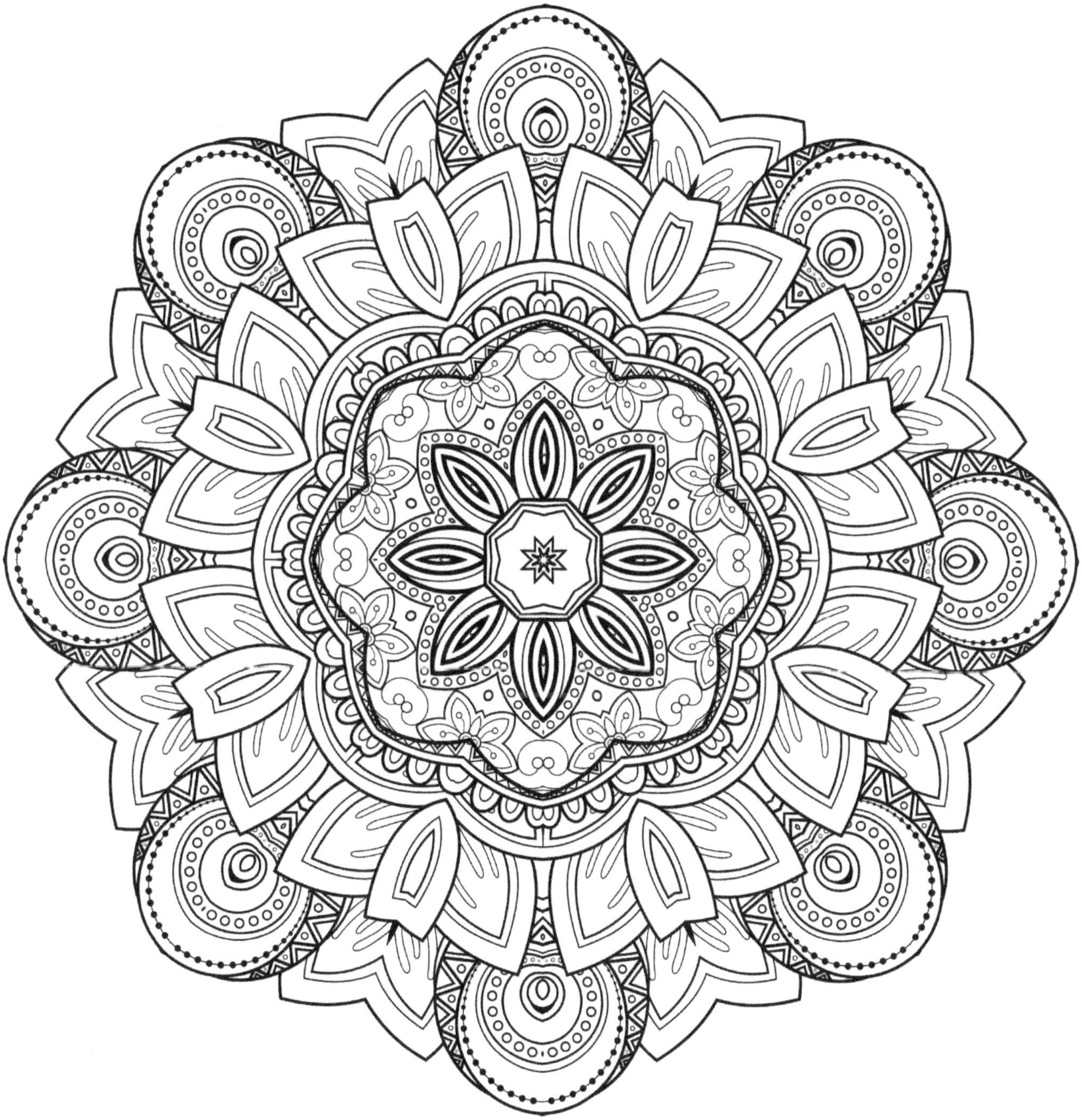

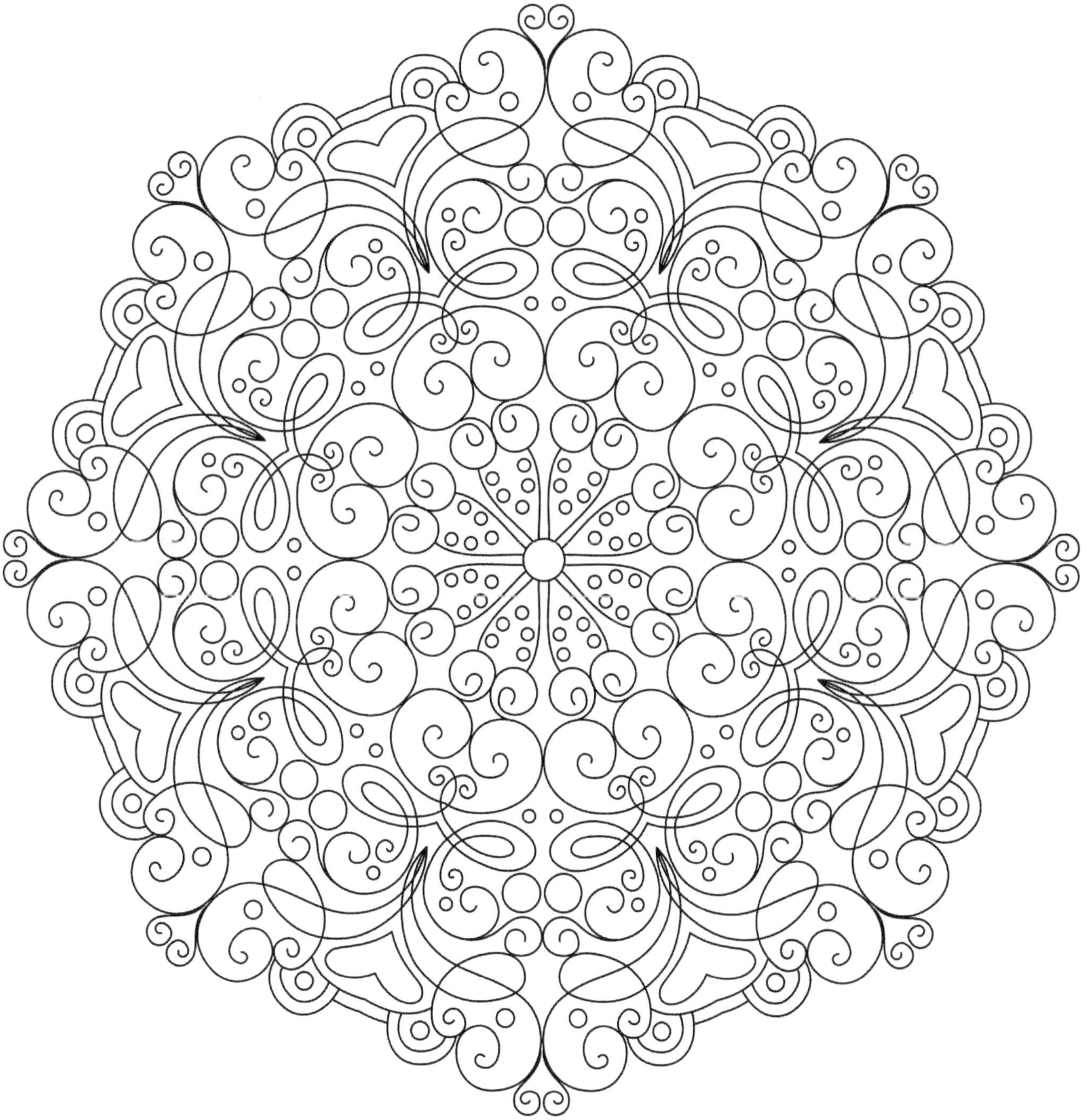

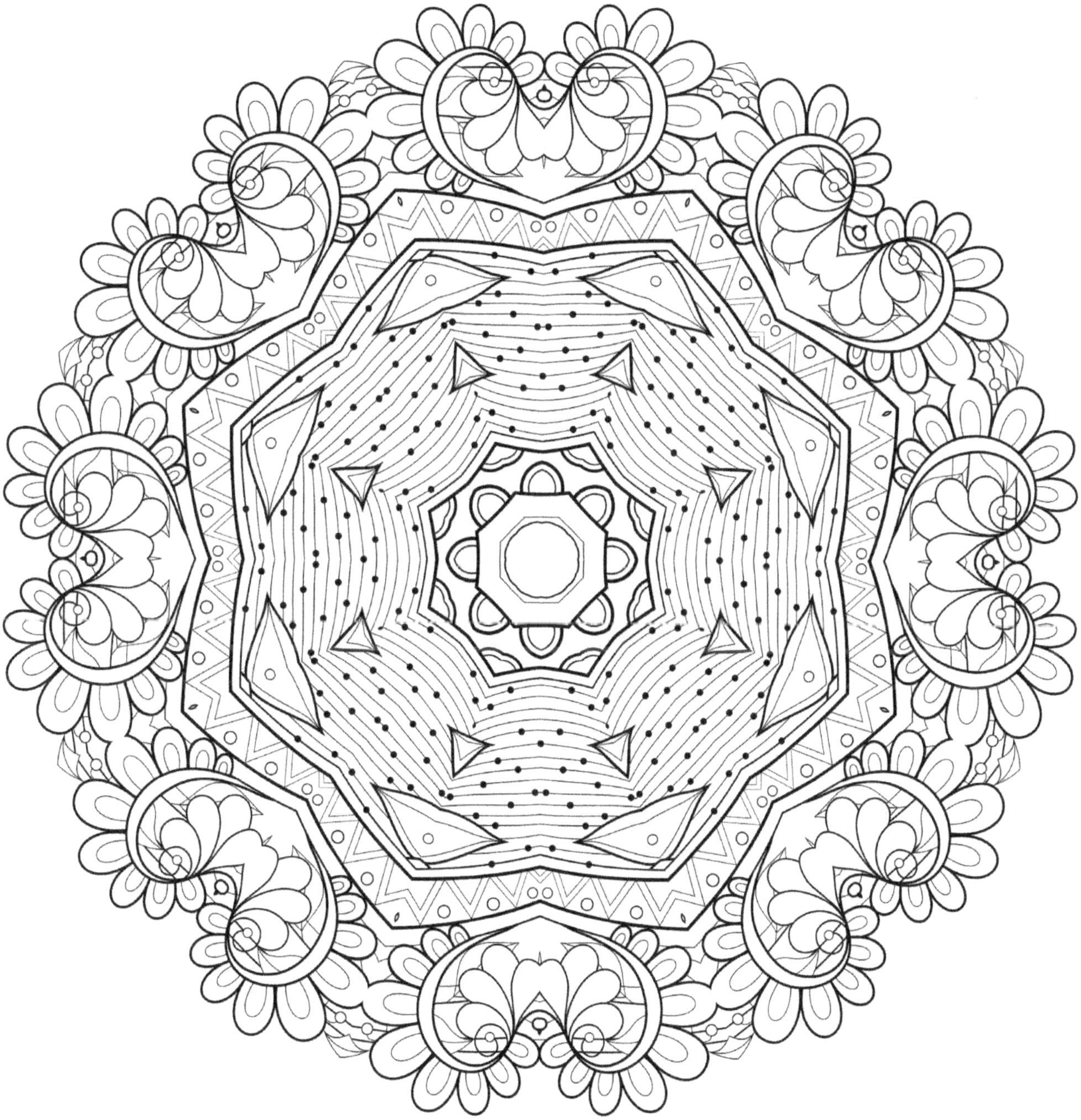

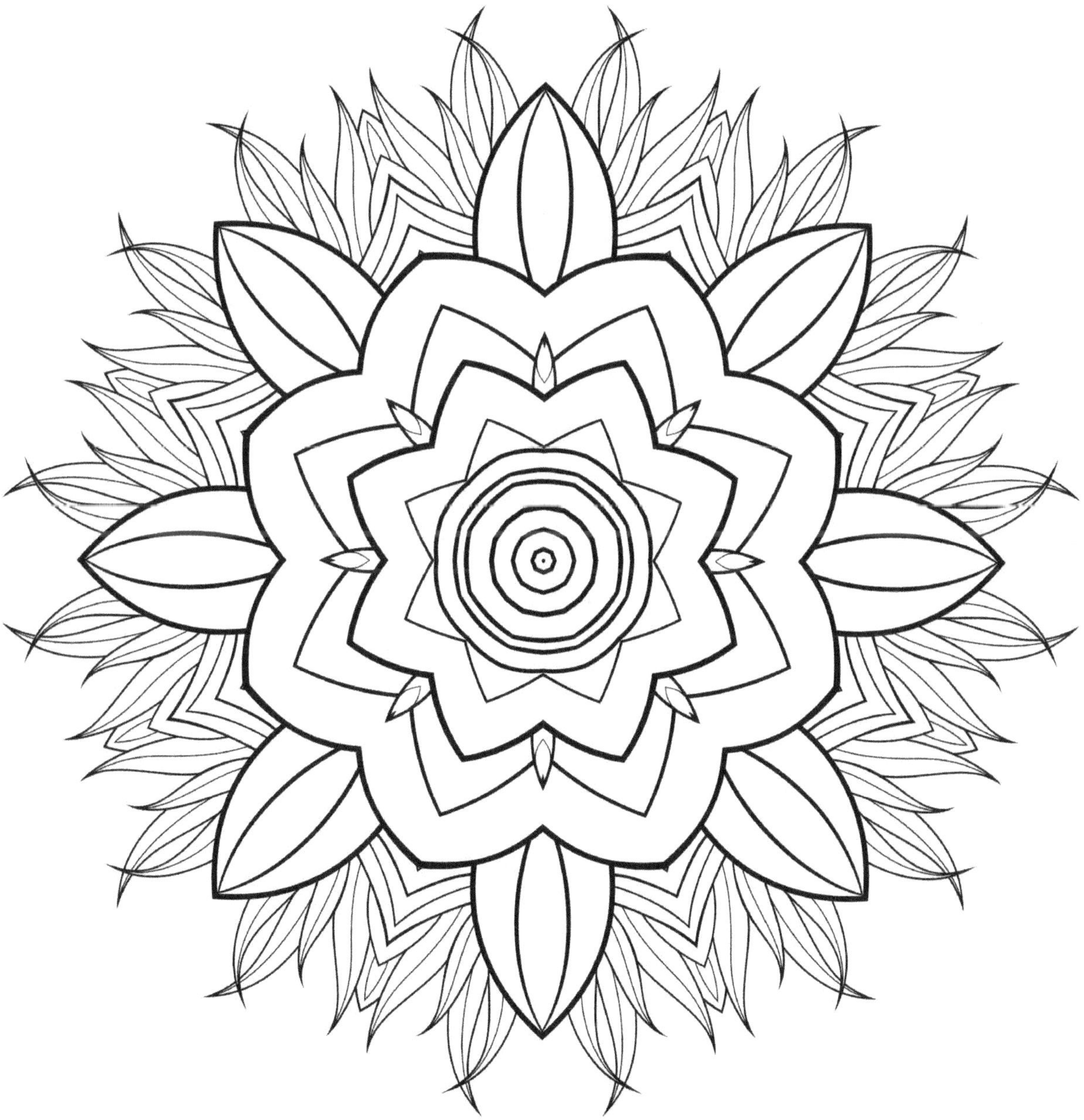

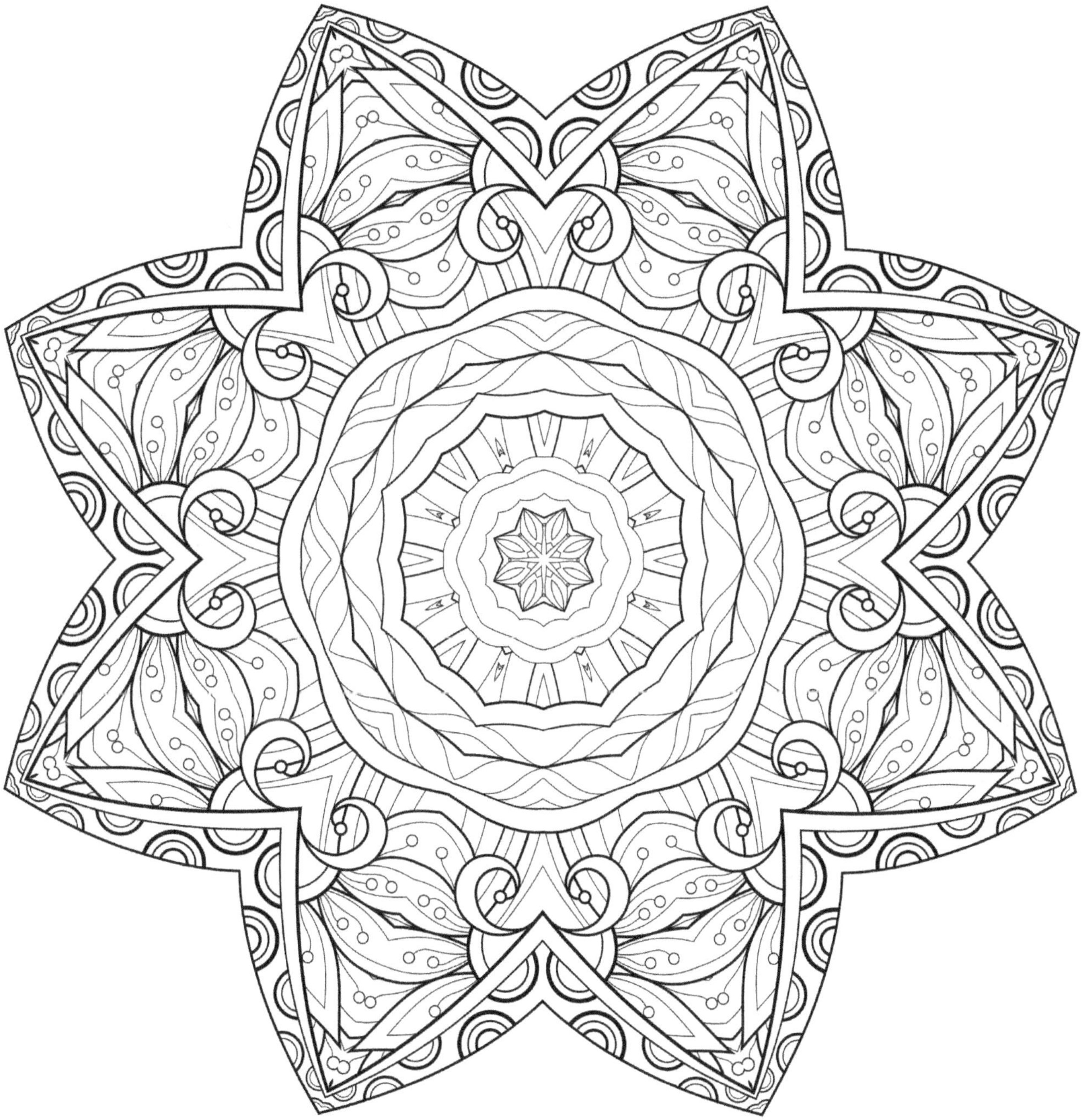

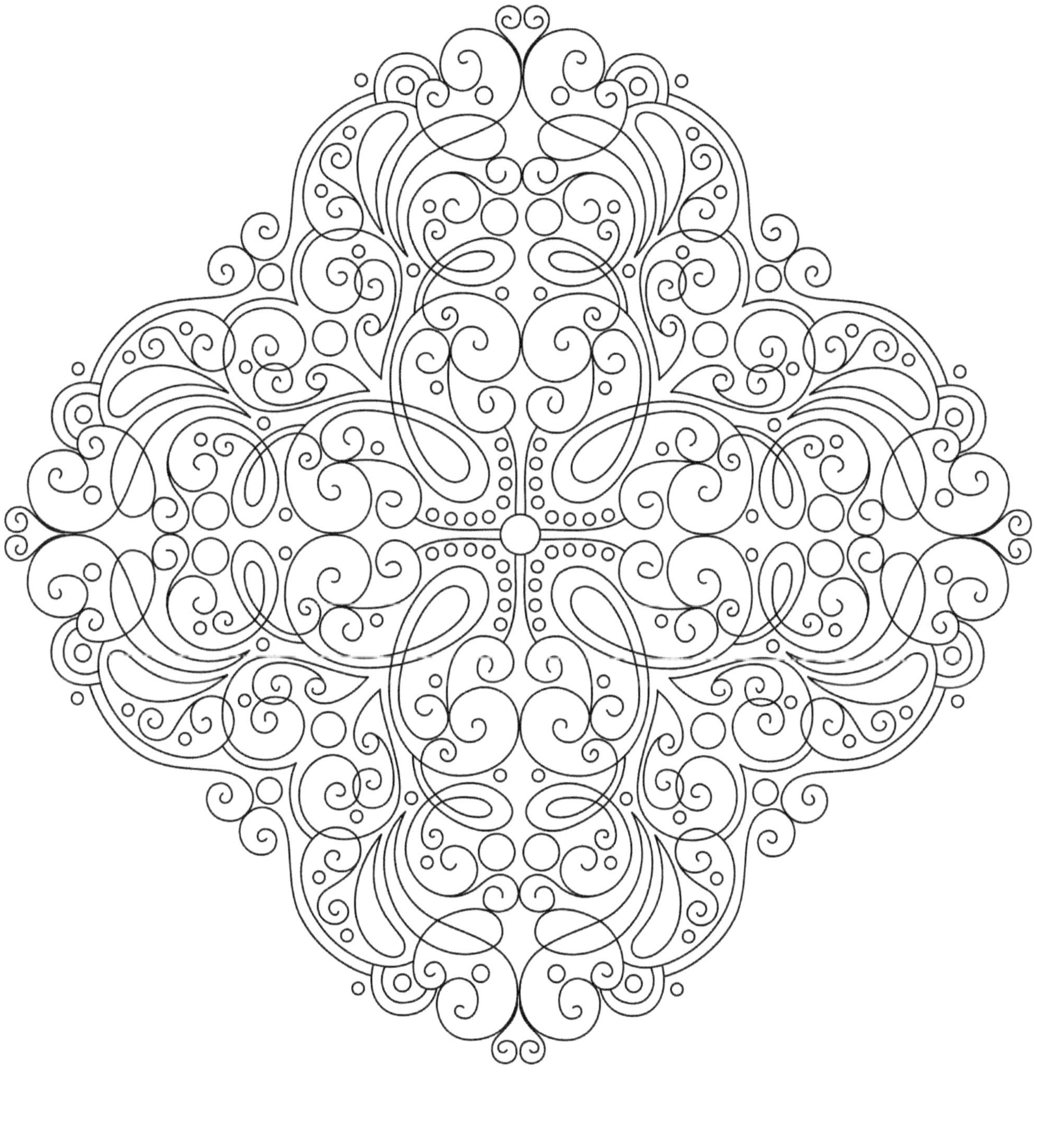

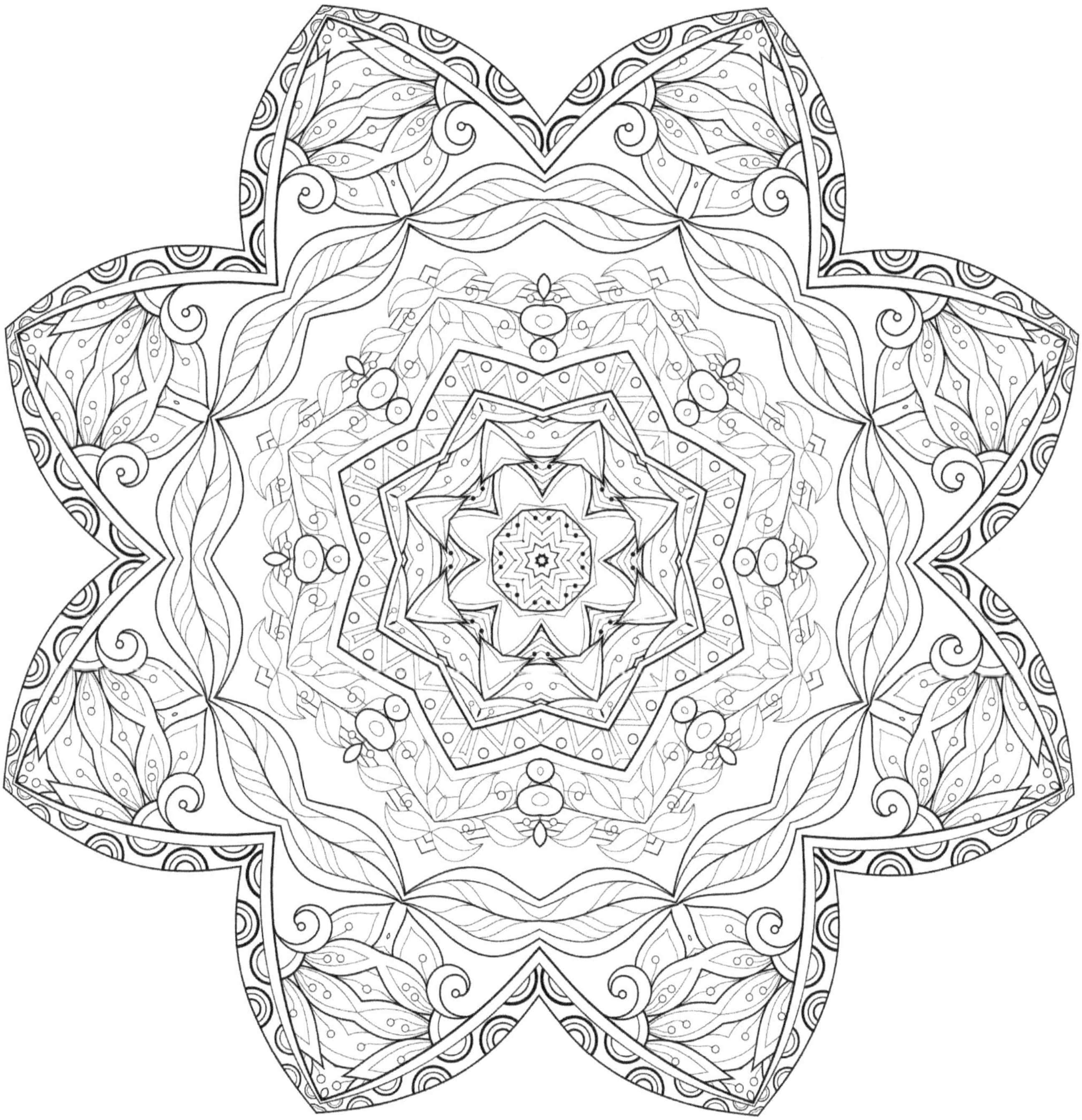

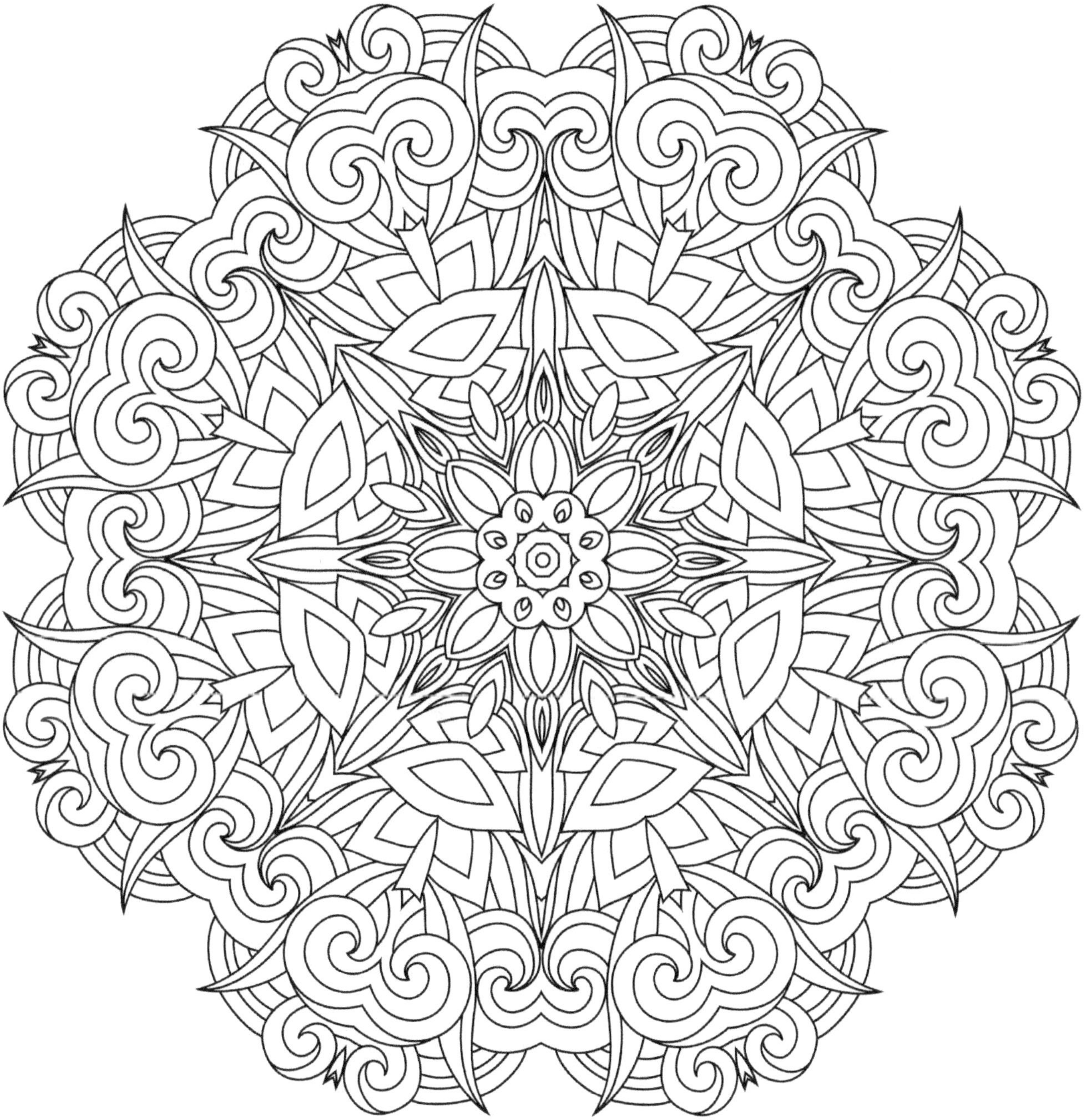

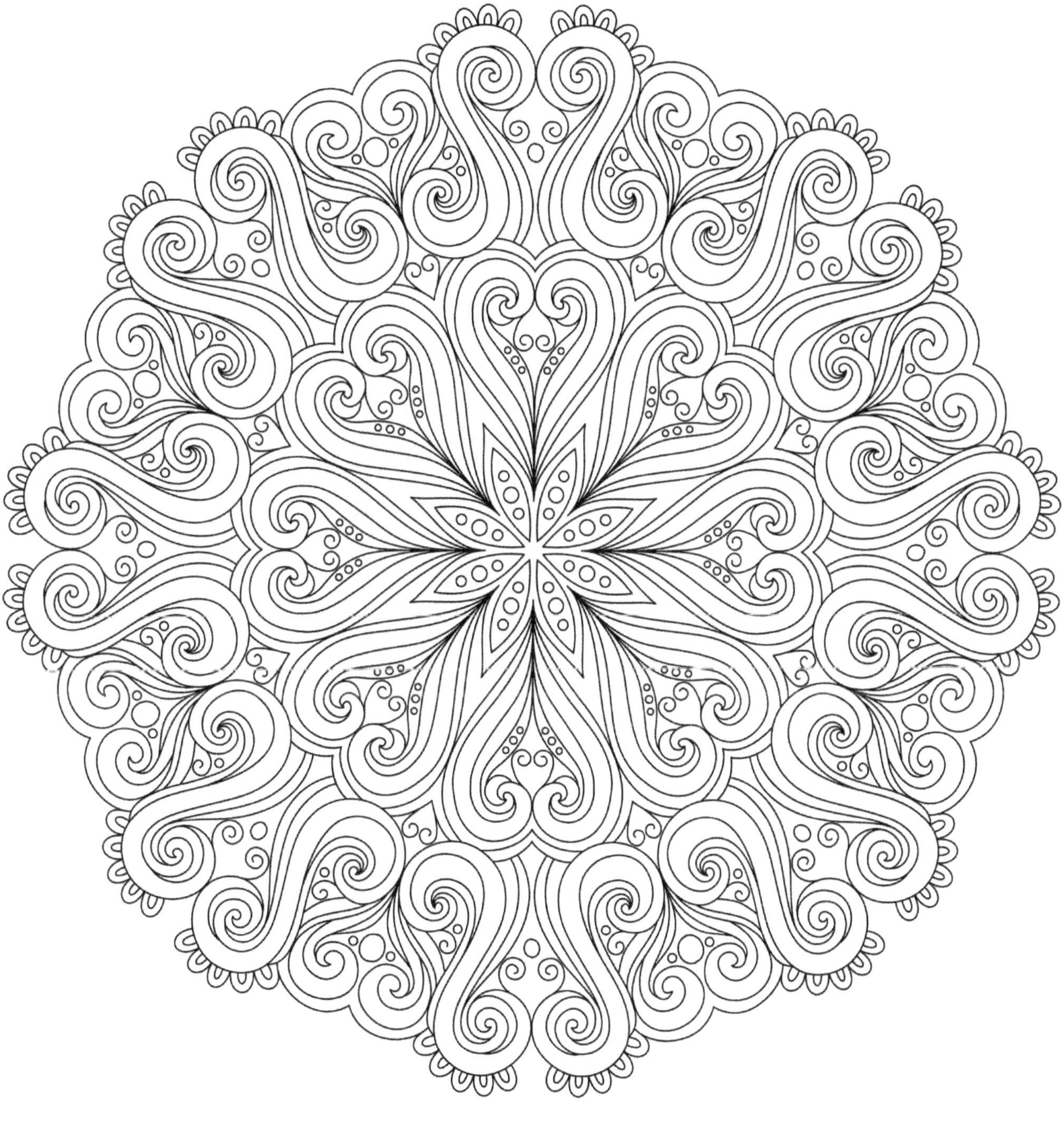

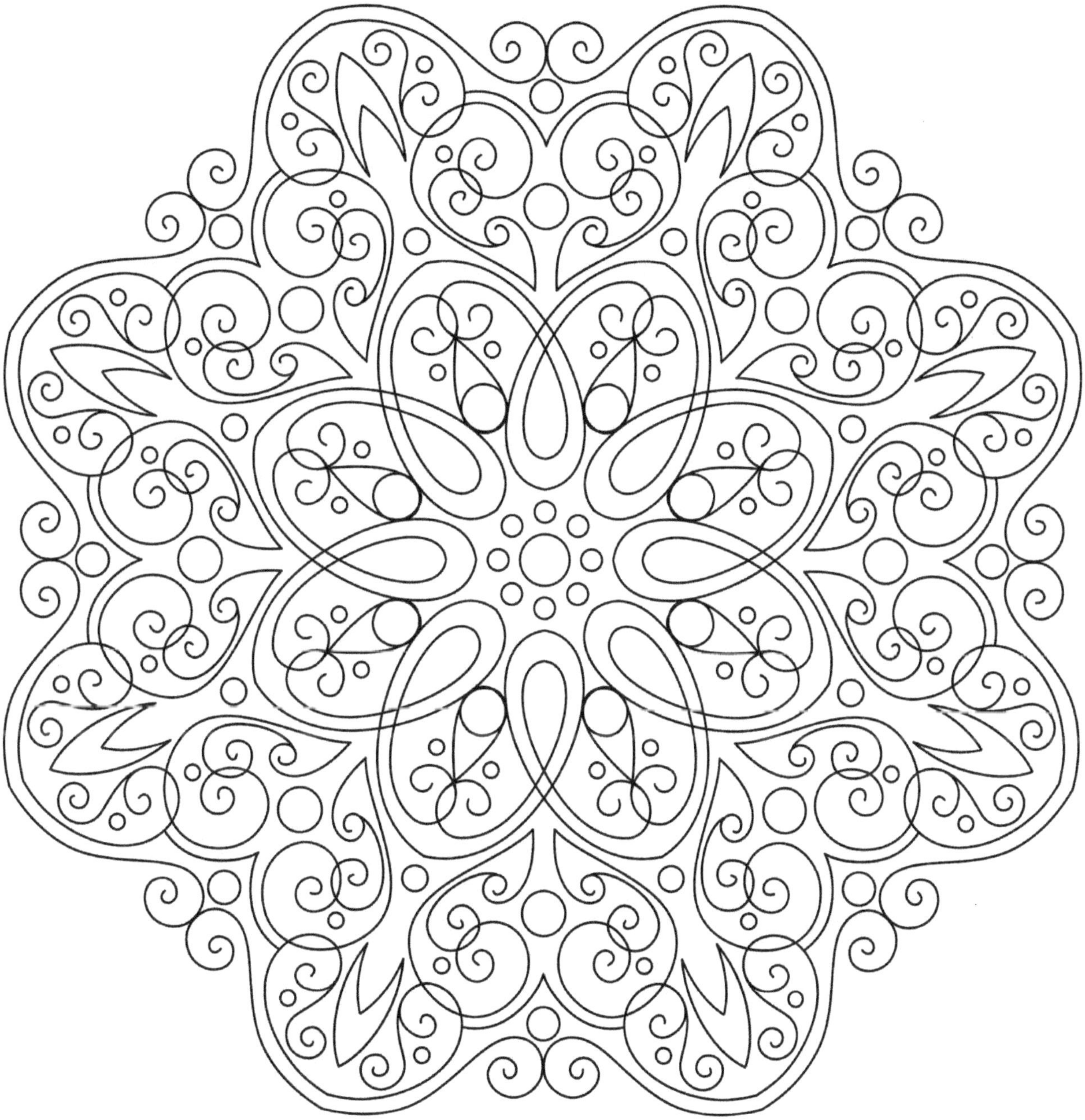

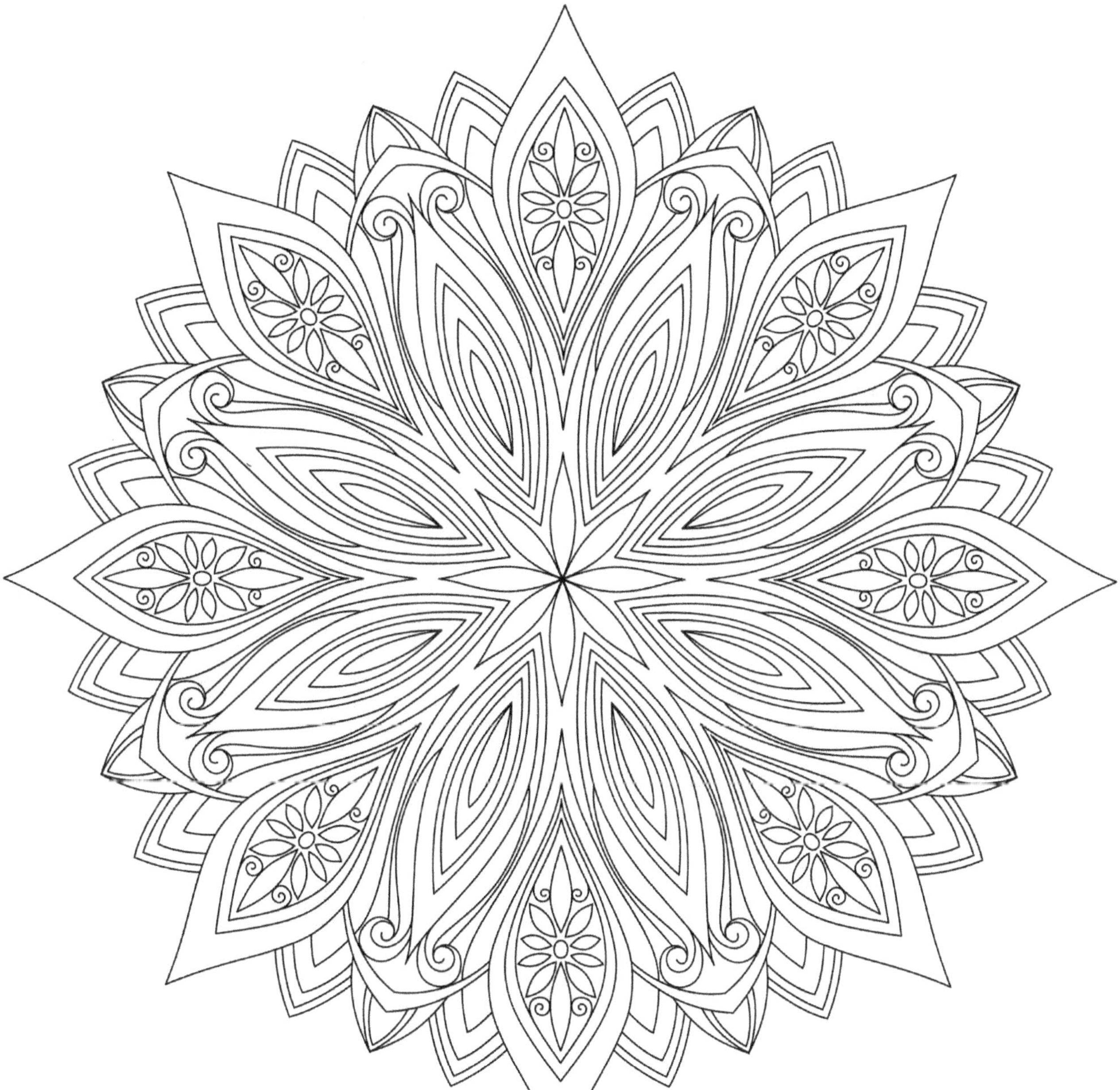

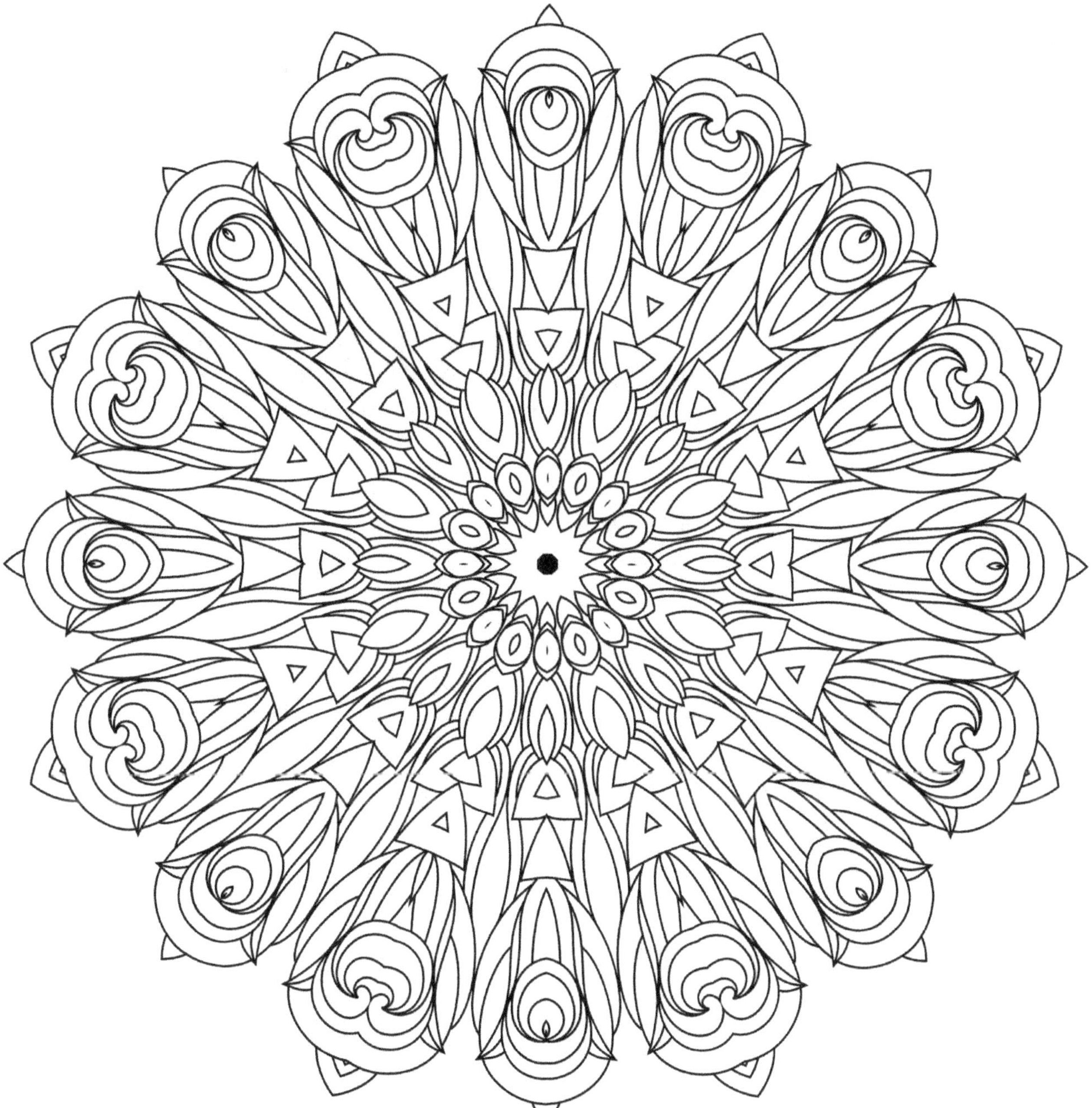

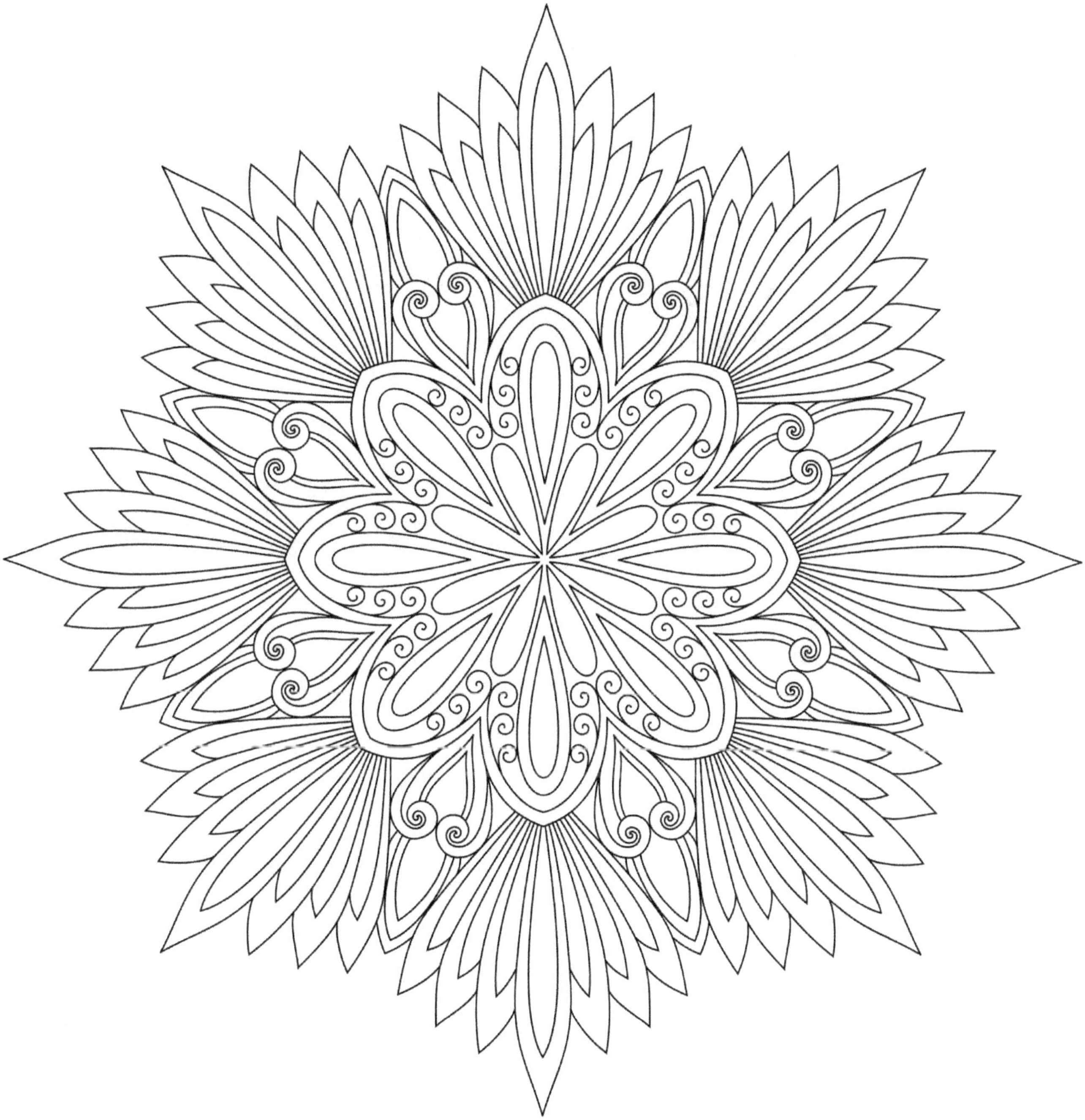

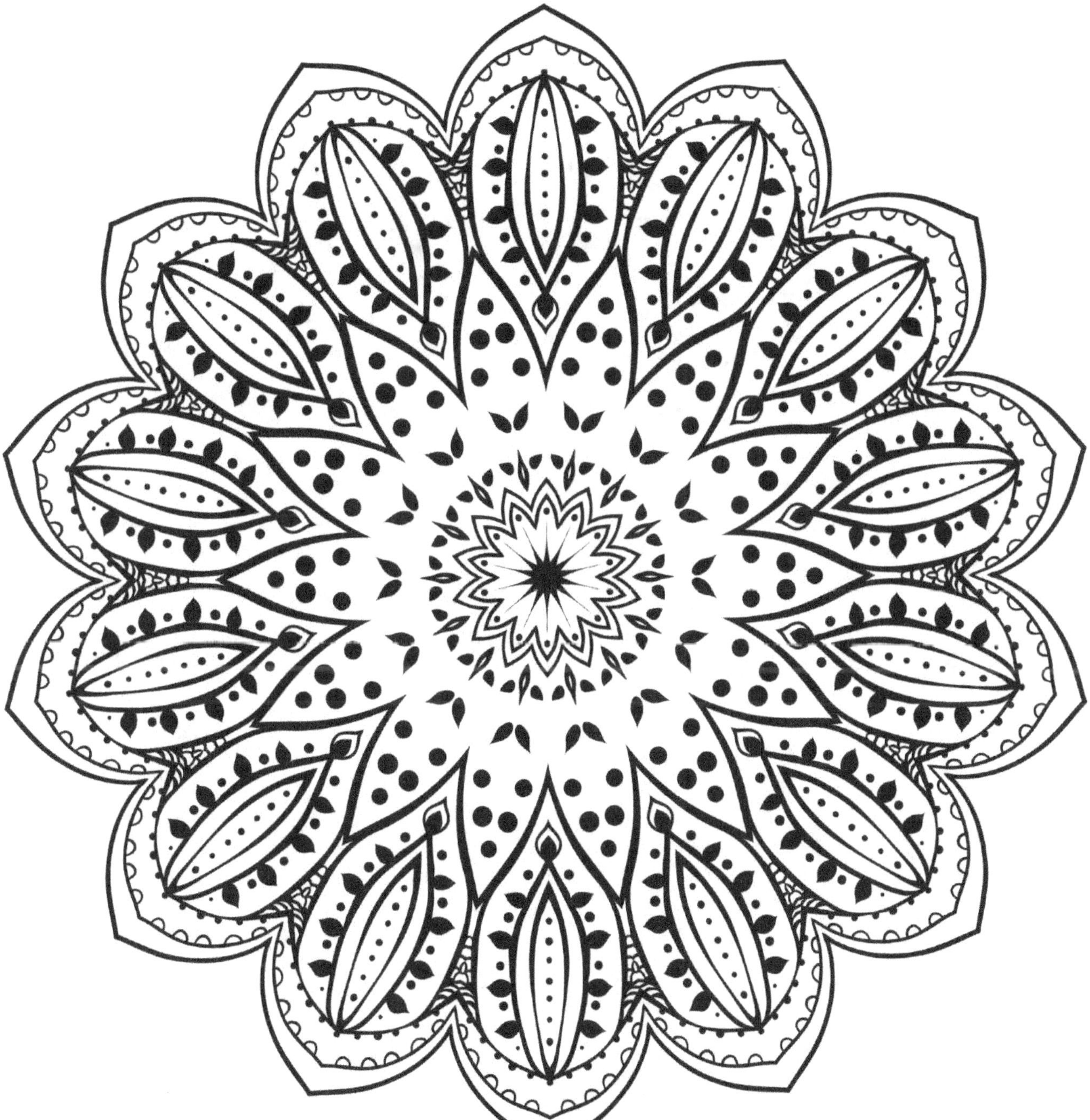

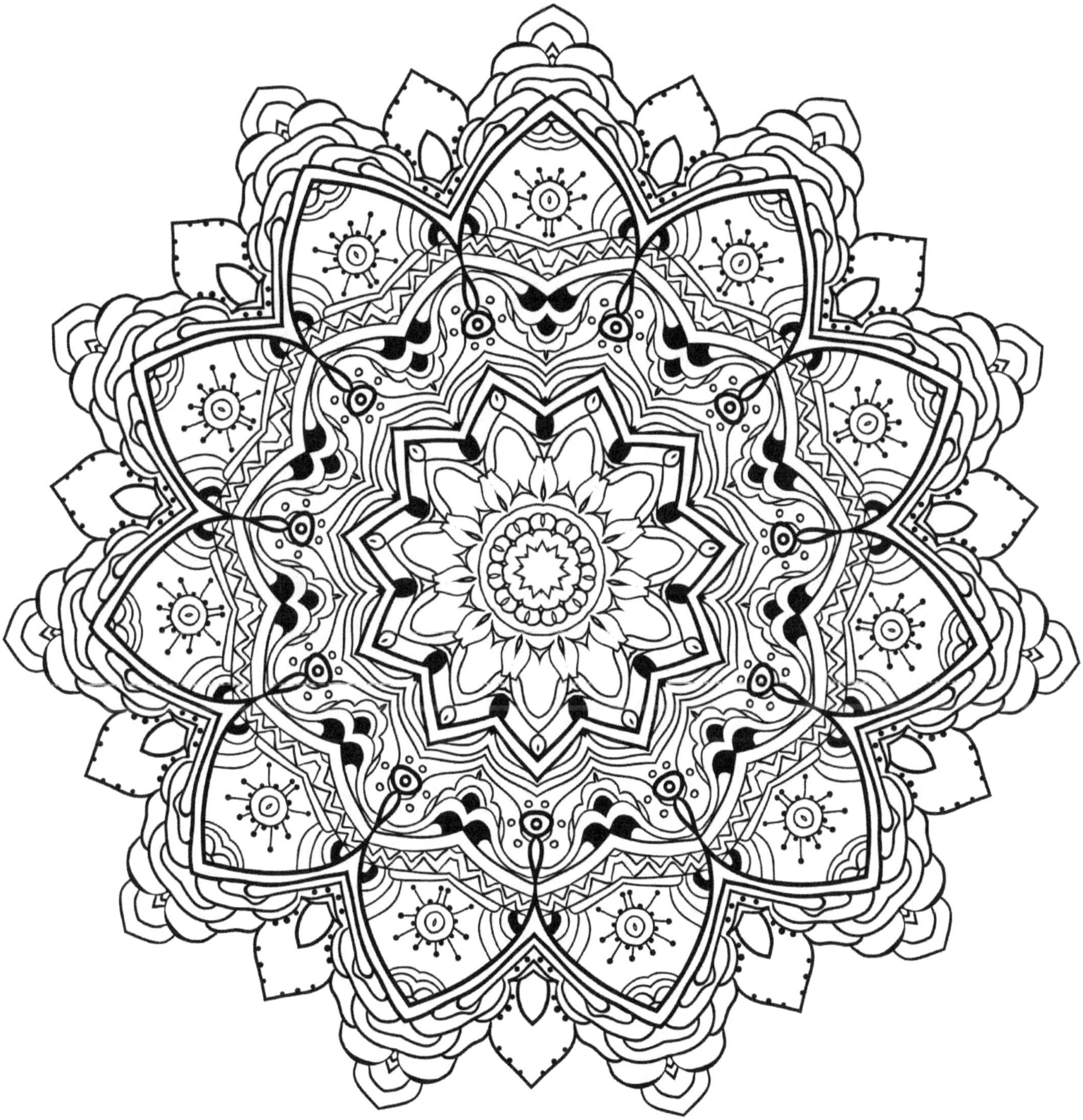

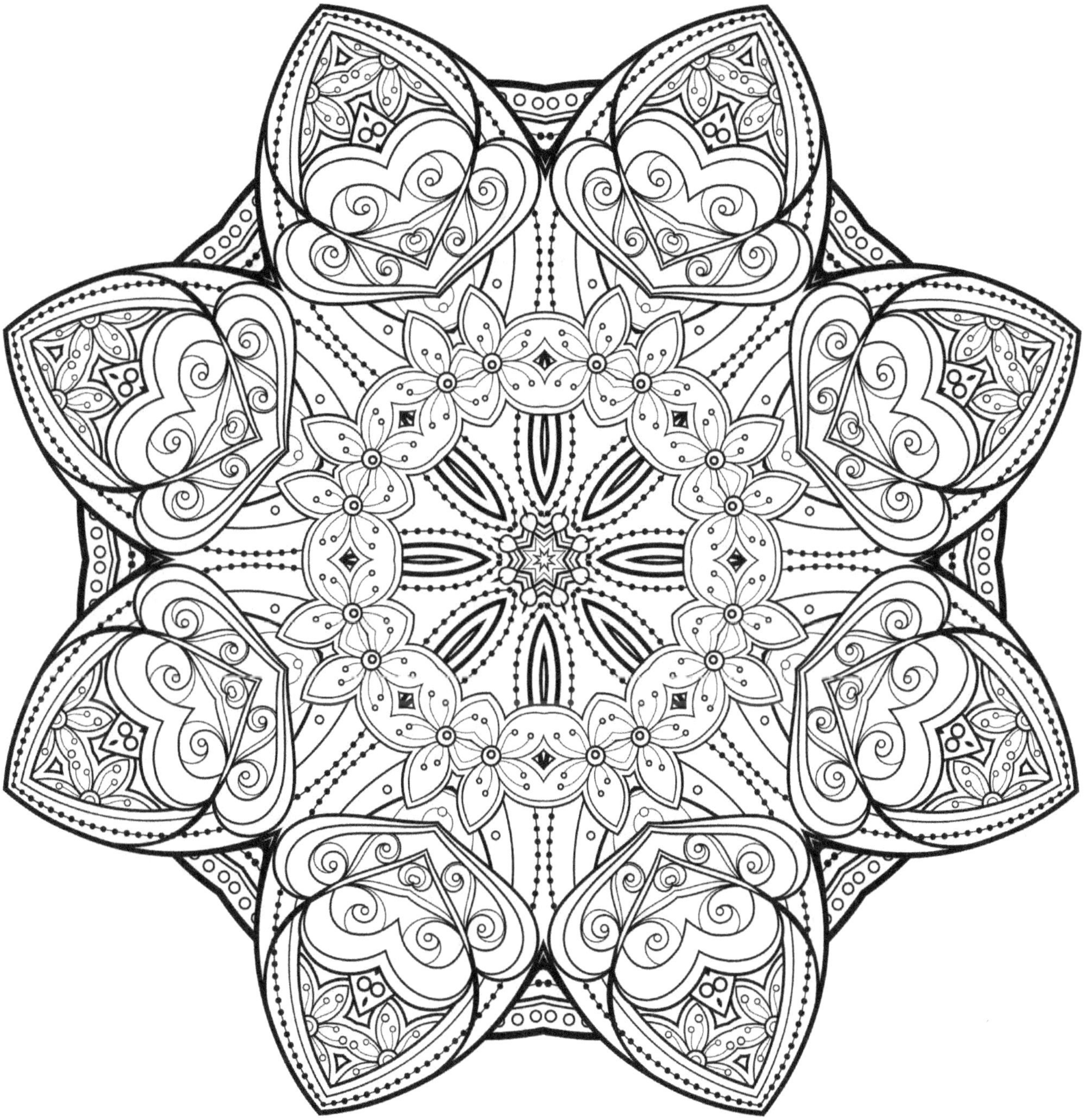

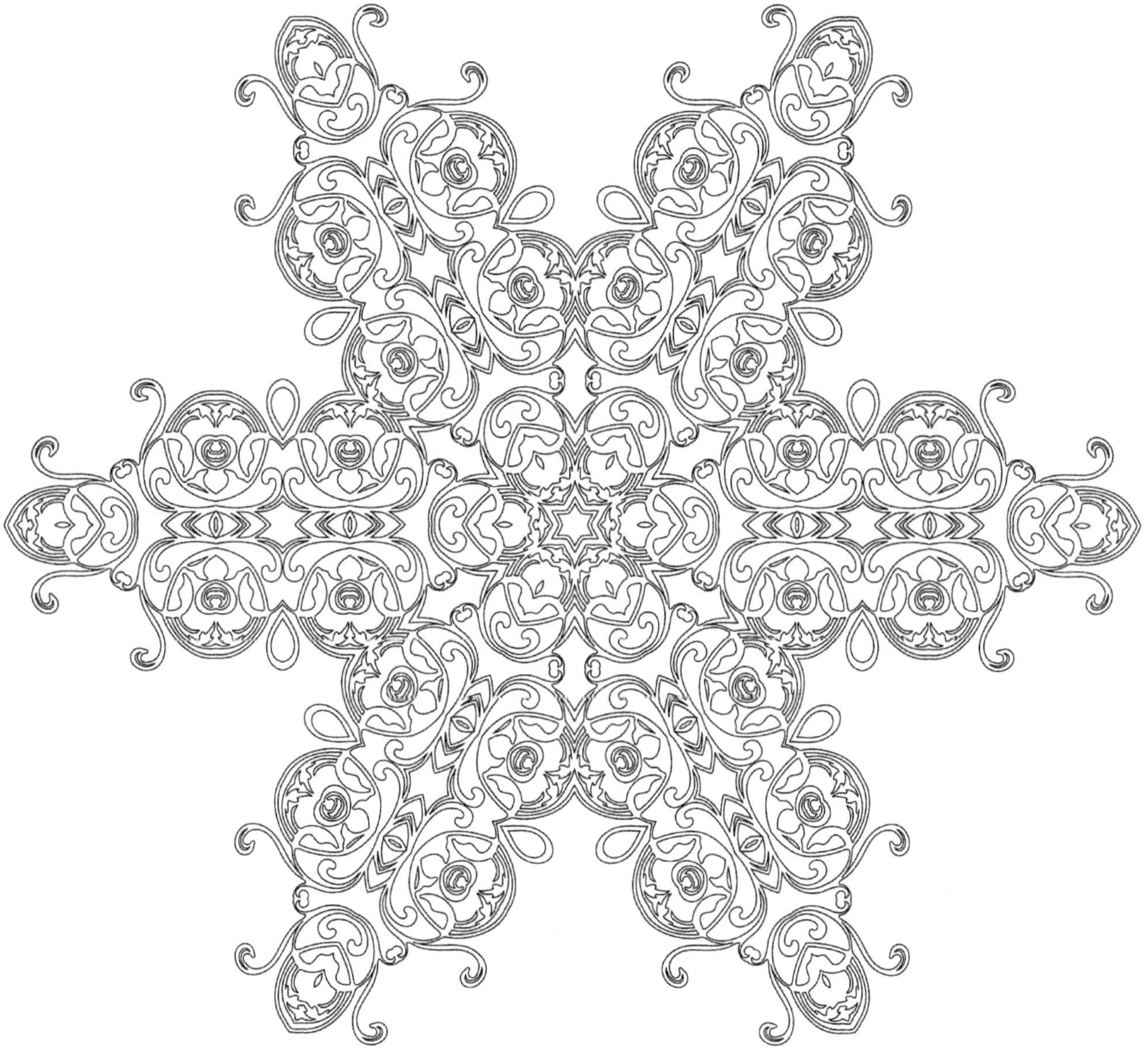

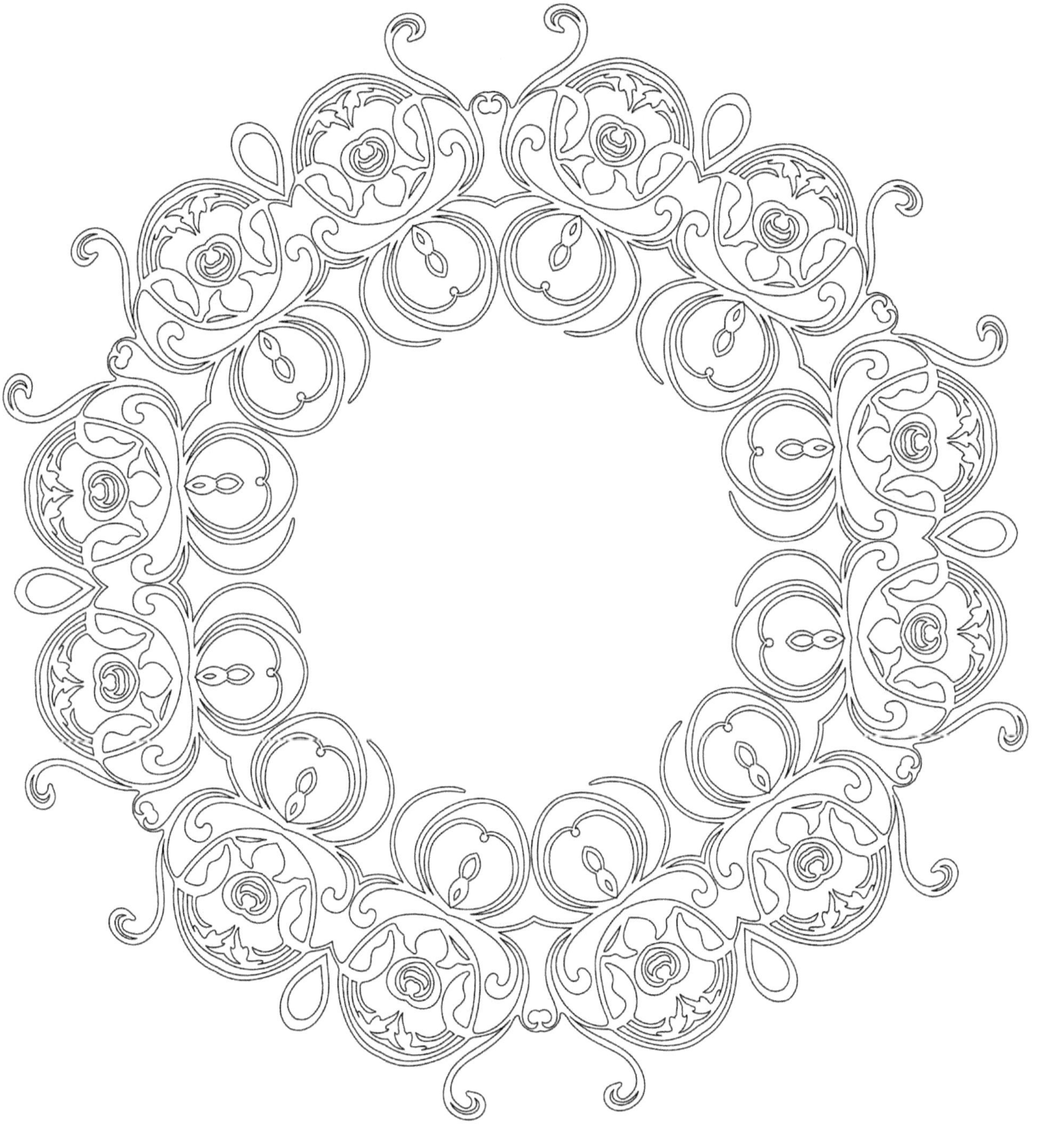

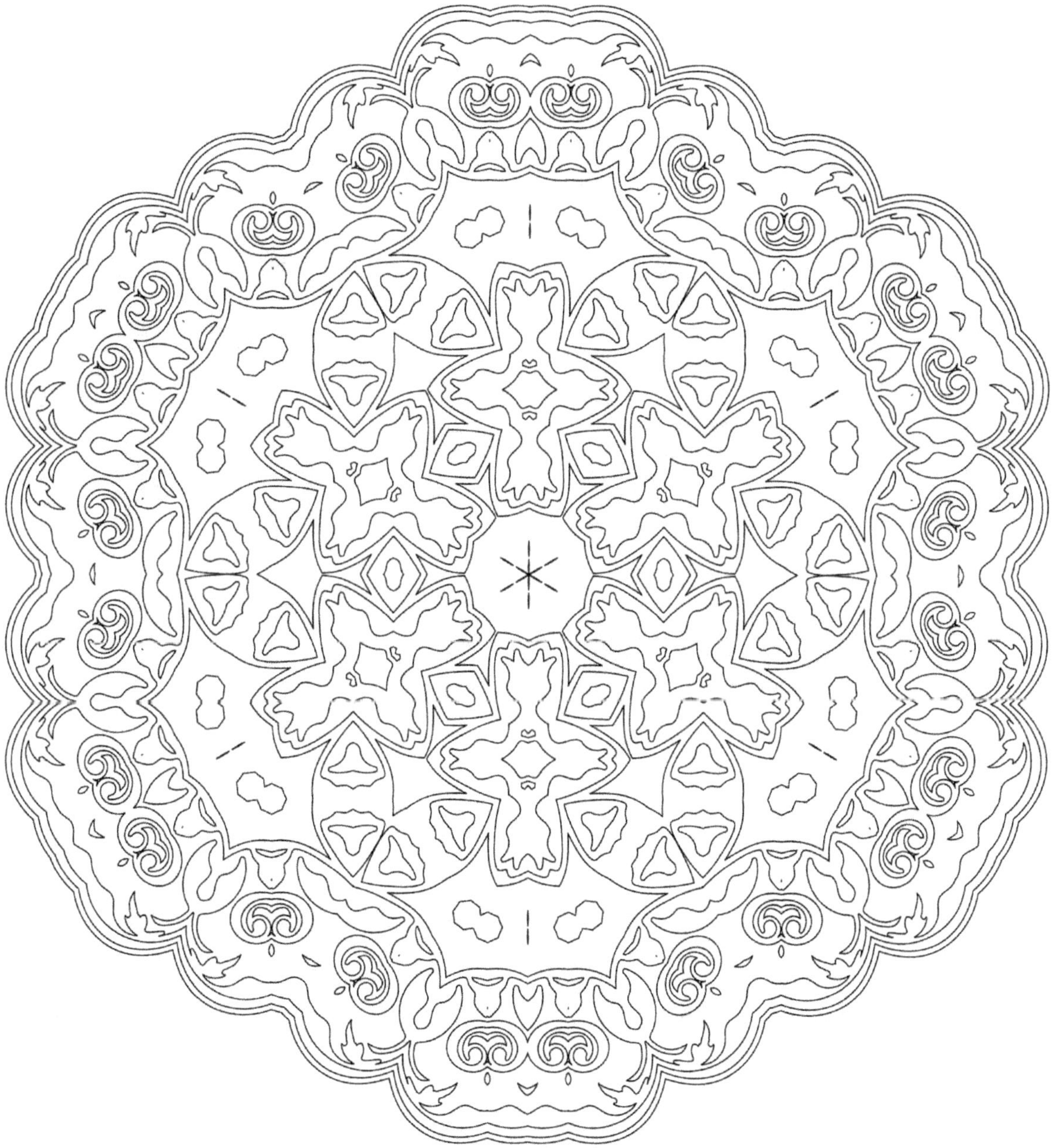

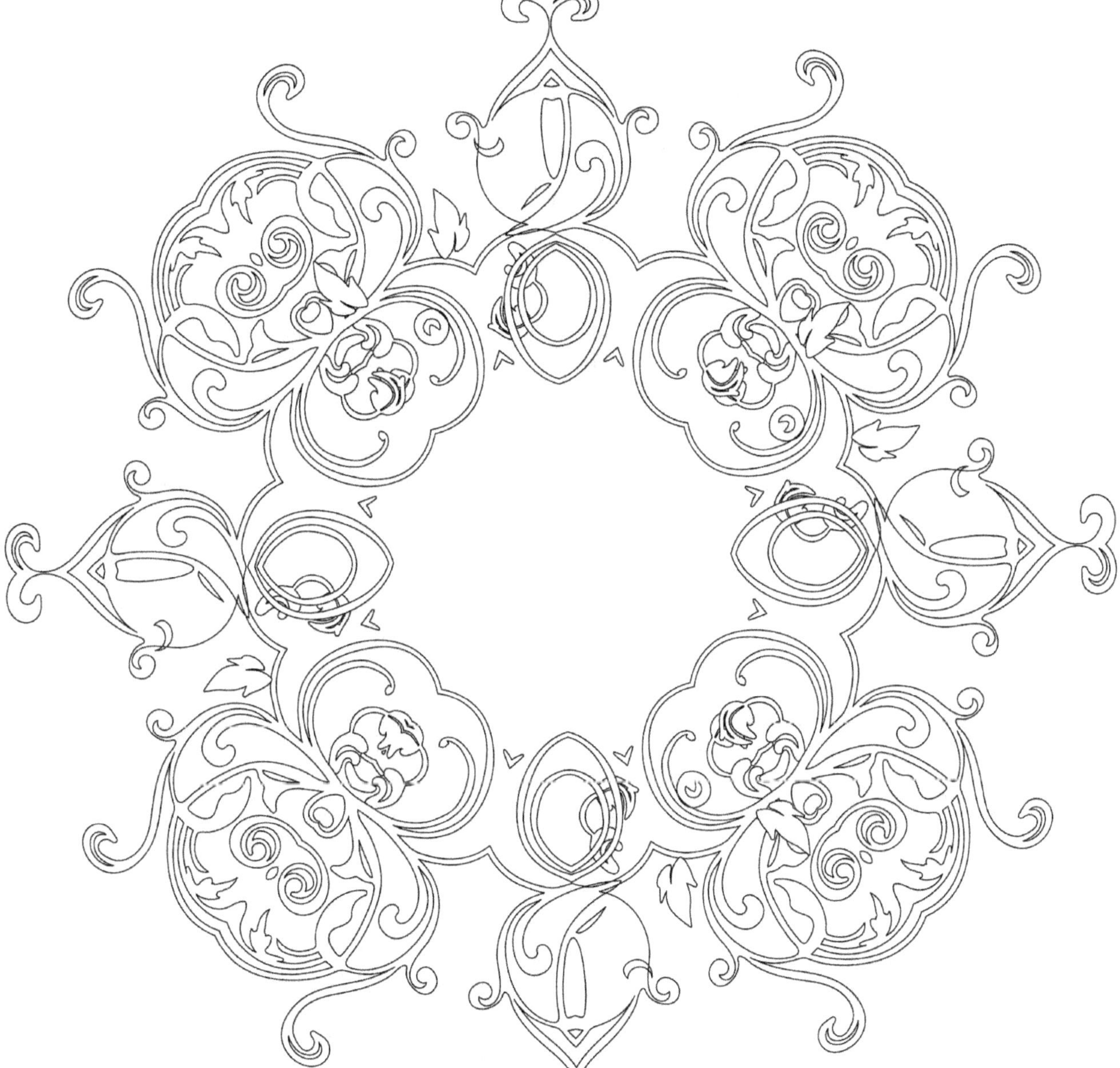

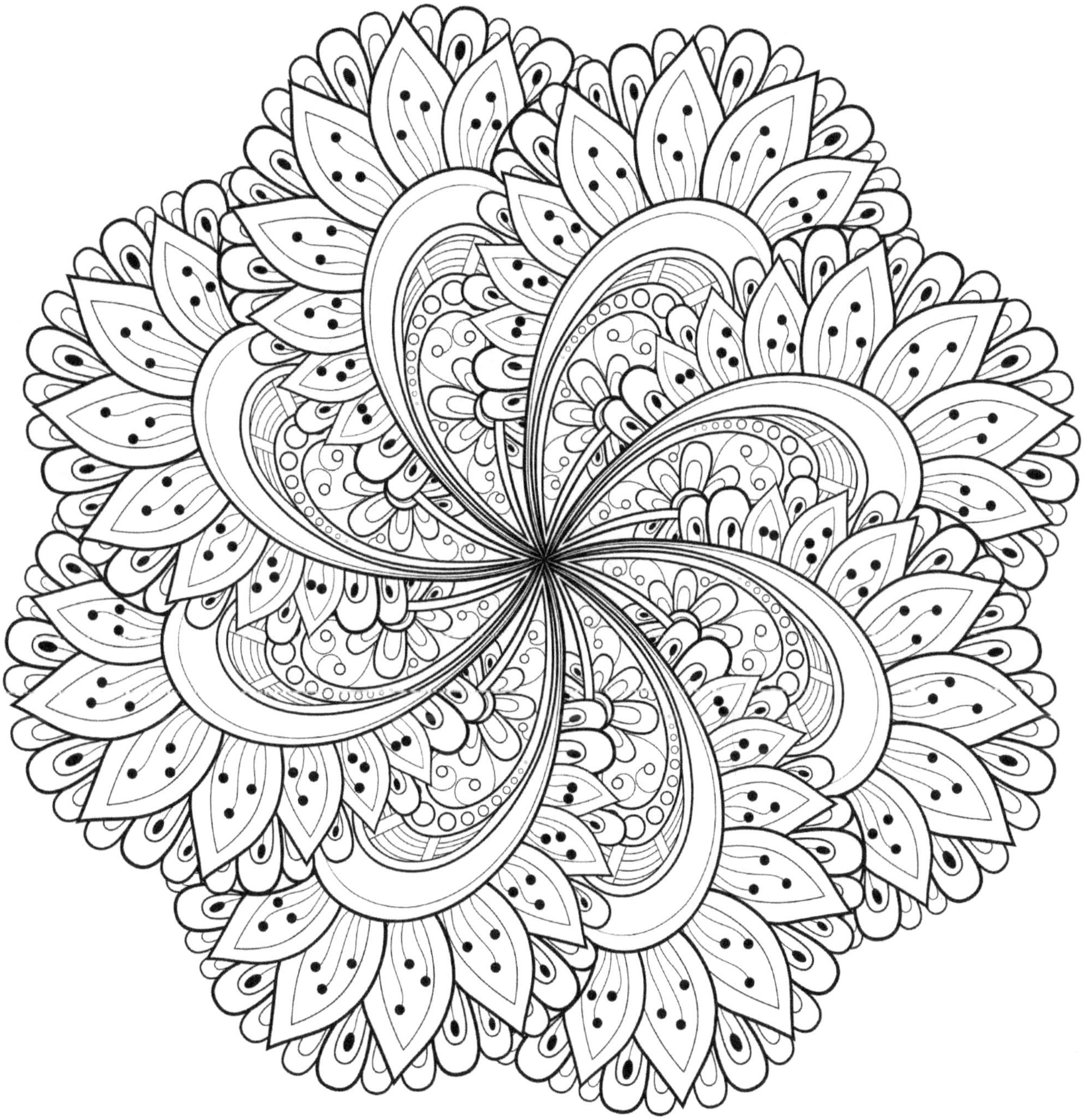

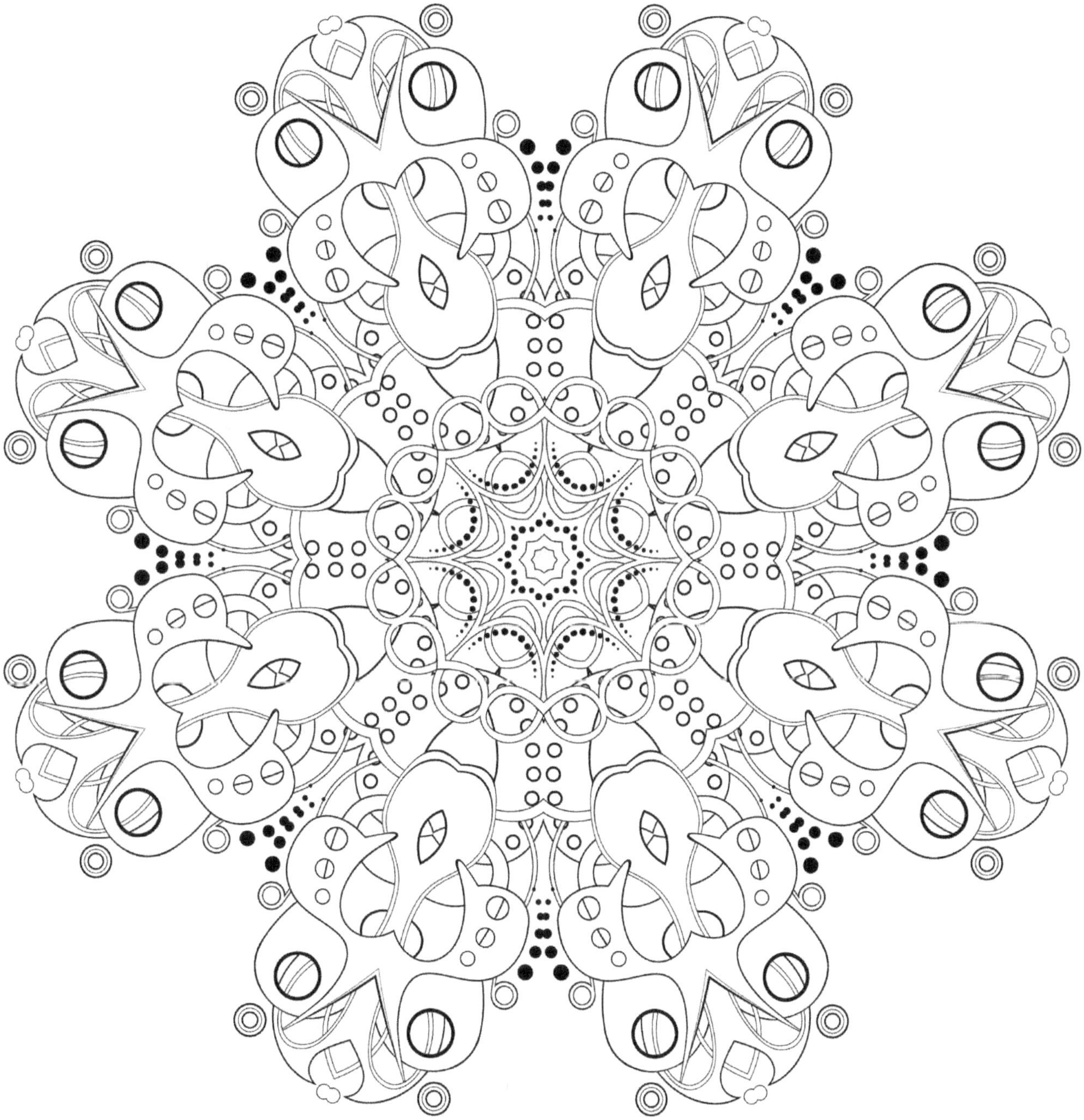

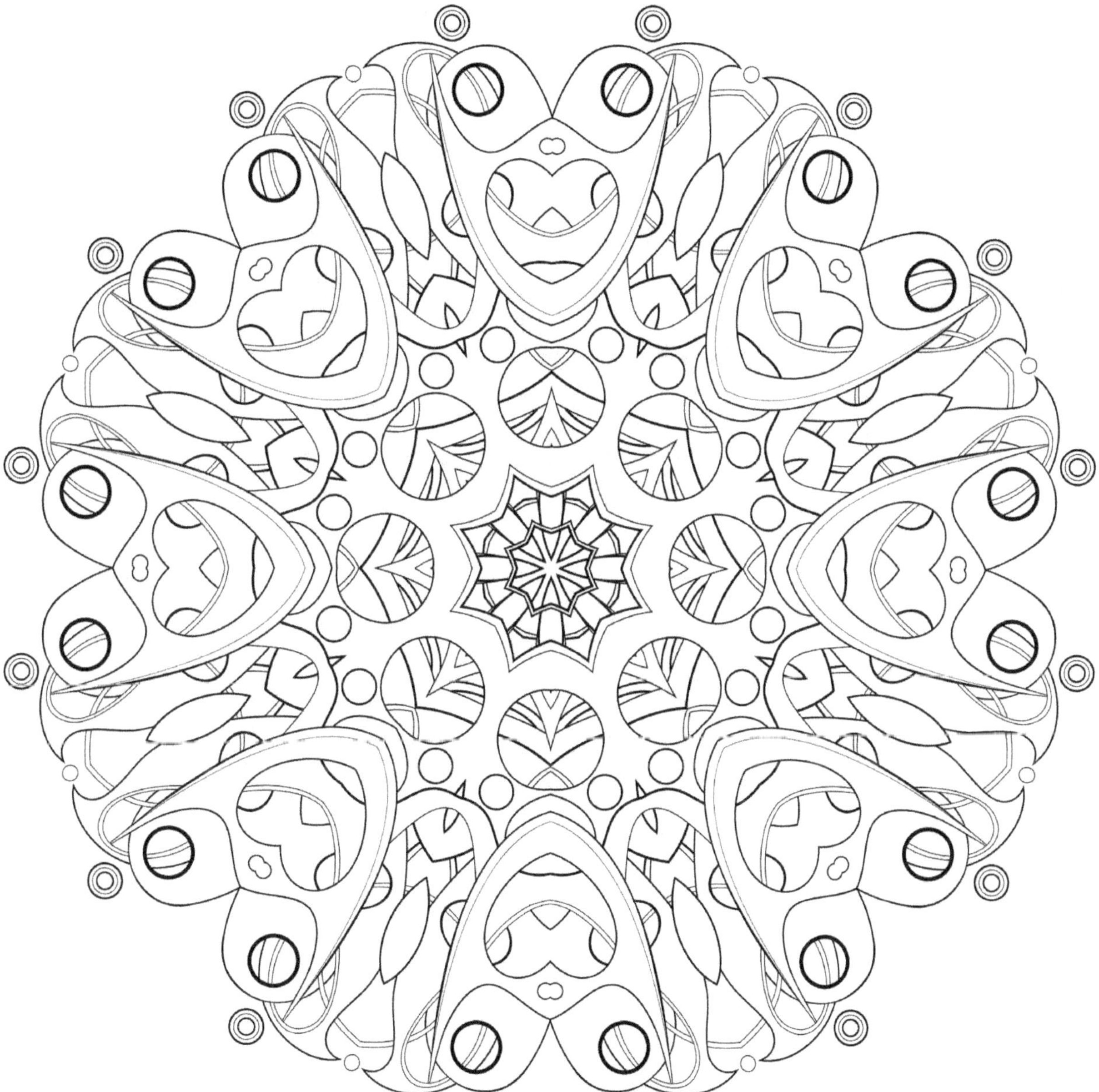

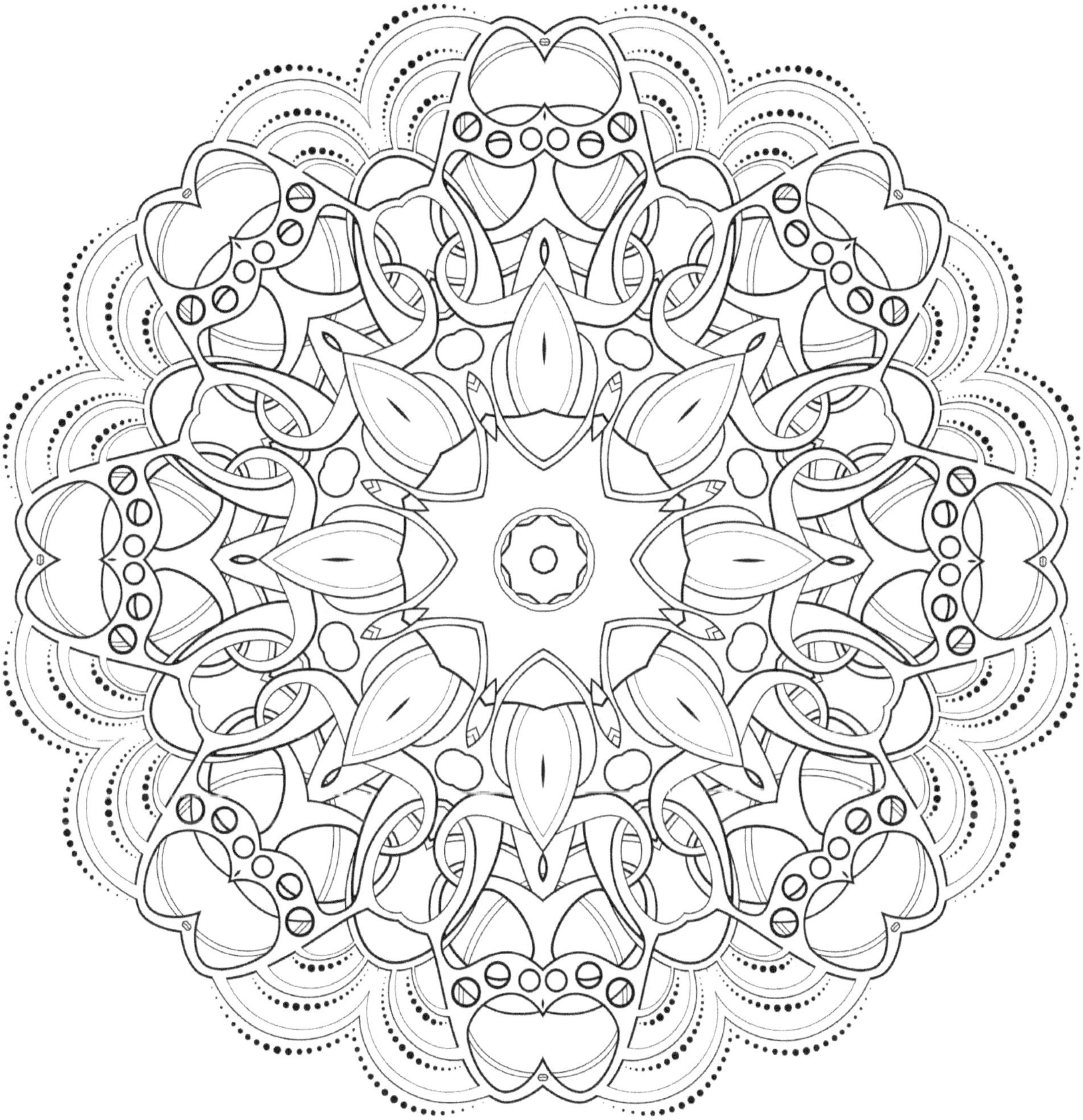

Hope you enjoy this coloring book.

Thank you.

www.ingramcontent.com/pod-product-compliance
Lightning Source LLC
Chambersburg PA
CBHW080835180526
45168CB00006B/2697